Samsung
Galaxy Tab®S

FOR

DUMMIES®

A Wiley Brand

by Dan Gookin

Samsung Galaxy Tab® S For Dummies®

Published by: **John Wiley & Sons, Inc.,** 111 River Street, Hoboken, NJ 07030-5774, www.wiley.com

Copyright © 2015 by John Wiley & Sons, Inc., Hoboken, New Jersey

Media and software compilation copyright © 2015 by John Wiley & Sons, Inc. All rights reserved.

Published simultaneously in Canada

No part of this publication may be reproduced, stored in a retrieval system or transmitted in any form or by any means, electronic, mechanical, photocopying, recording, scanning or otherwise, except as permitted under Sections 107 or 108 of the 1976 United States Copyright Act, without the prior written permission of the Publisher. Requests to the Publisher for permission should be addressed to the Permissions Department, John Wiley & Sons, Inc., 111 River Street, Hoboken, NJ 07030, (201) 748-6011, fax (201) 748-6008, or online at http://www.wiley.com/go/permissions.

Trademarks: Wiley, For Dummies, the Dummies Man logo, Dummies.com, Making Everything Easier, and related trade dress are trademarks or registered trademarks of John Wiley & Sons, Inc. and may not be used without written permission. Samsung Galaxy Tab is a registered trademark of Samsung Electronics Co. Ltd. All other trademarks are the property of their respective owners. John Wiley & Sons, Inc. is not associated with any product or vendor mentioned in this book.

For general information on our other products and services, please contact our Customer Care Department within the U.S. at 877-762-2974, outside the U.S. at 317-572-3993, or fax 317-572-4002. For technical support, please visit www.wiley.com/techsupport.

Wiley publishes in a variety of print and electronic formats and by print-on-demand. Some material included with standard print versions of this book may not be included in e-books or in print-on-demand. If this book refers to media such as a CD or DVD that is not included in the version you purchased, you may download this material at http://booksupport.wiley.com. For more information about Wiley products, visit www.wiley.com.

Library of Congress Control Number: 2014948517

ISBN 978-1-119-00574-2 (pbk); 978-1-119-00582-7 (ebk); ISBN 978-1-119-00579-7 (ebk)

Manufactured in the United States of America

10 9 8 7 6 5 4 3 2 1

Contents at a Glance

Table of Contents

Introduction

The Samsung Galaxy Tab is an excellent choice for your twenty-first century, mobile digital life. The tablet is a remarkable gizmo, one that's capable of doing so much. Samsung packed a lot of potential into the device. One thing they didn't pack were any instructions. Yes, despite its impressive power, the Galaxy Tab can be a confusing, intimidating piece of hardware.

Relax.

You hold in your hand a great resource, companion, and guide to your Galaxy Tab. The purpose here is to help you get the most from your tablet, without scaring the bejeebers out of you.

About This Book

Still reading? Great! So few people bother with the introduction in any book that I'm amazed you bothered to keep going. Honestly, I could write down how to turn lead into gold in this paragraph and you'd be one of six people on the planet to ever read it. Count yourself fortunate. And handsome. I mean, why not?

This book is a reference. It's written to help you get the most from your Galactic tablet. Each chapter covers a specific topic, and the sections in each chapter address an issue related to the topic. The overall idea is to show how to do things on the tablet and to help you get the most from it without over-whelming you with information or intimidating you into despair.

Sample sections in this book include

- ✔ Making a home for the tablet
- ✔ Touring the Home screen
- ✔ Typing quickly by using predictive text
- ✔ Placing a Skype phone call
- ✔ Running Facebook on your tablet

> ✔ Recording video
>
> ✔ Turning lead into gold
>
> ✔ Finding your lost tablet

Did you notice that one of those items is fake? That's because you're still reading the Introduction and I'm proud of you for sticking with it.

This book explains all topics carefully. Everything is cross-referenced. Technical terms and topics, when they come up, are neatly shoved to the side, where they're easily avoided. The idea here isn't to learn anything. This book's philosophy is to help you look it up, figure it out, and get on with your life.

This book follows a few conventions for using a Galaxy Tab. First of all, I refer to your device as the *Galaxy Tab* or just *Tab* throughout the book. I might also write *Galaxy tablet* or even, occasionally, *Galactic tablet*. Generally speaking, all the information here applies to the Galaxy Tab S and the Galaxy Tab 4. Occasionally, I'll offer specific information when the tablets differ in features or methods.

The way you interact with the tablet is by using its *touchscreen*. The device also has some physical buttons, found below the touchscreen. It also features some holes and connectors. All those items are described in Chapter 1. You can touch the screen in various ways, which are explained and named in Chapter 3.

Chapter 4 discusses tablet text input, which involves using an onscreen keyboard. You can also input text by speaking to the tablet, which is also covered in Chapter 4.

This book directs you to do things by following numbered steps. Each step involves a specific activity, such as touching something on the screen; for example:

2. Choose Downloads.

This step directs you to touch the text or item labeled *Downloads* on the screen. You might also be told to do this:

3. Tap Downloads.

 Some options can be turned off or on, as indicated by a box with a check mark in it, similar to what's shown in the margin. Tap the box to add or remove the check mark. When the check mark appears, the option is on; otherwise, it's off.

Some on-off features are activated by using a Master Control icon, similar to what's shown in the margin. When the button is green, the feature is on. You can either touch the icon or slide it a wee bit by dragging your finger on the touchscreen.

Foolish Assumptions

Even though this book is written with the gentle handholding required by anyone who is just starting out or who is easily intimidated, I've made a few assumptions. For example, I assume that you're a human being and not the emperor of Jupiter. See? You're getting all this comedy gold just from sticking to reading the Introduction. (I'm gonna write my mom about this.)

My biggest assumption: You have a Samsung Galaxy tablet, either a Tab S or a Tab 4. This book covers both. The Tabs come in a variety of sizes. The only difference relevant to this book is whether you hold the device vertically or horizontally. Even that doesn't matter much in the big picture.

A Tab that accesses the mobile data (cellular) network is called an LTE Tab, where LTE stands for Long Term Evolution or something. It doesn't matter. The other Tab is known as a Wi-Fi-only tab. Any differences between the two types of Tabs are pointed out in the text.

You don't need a computer to use this book, although having one does let you do certain things. The computer can be a desktop or a laptop, and a PC or a Macintosh. Oh, I suppose it could also be a Linux computer. In any event, I refer to the computer as "a computer" throughout this book. When directions are specific to a PC or a Mac, the book says so.

Finally, this book doesn't assume that you have a Google account, but having one helps. Information is provided in Chapter 2 about setting up a Google account — an extremely important part of using the Galaxy Tab. Having a Google account opens up a slew of useful features, information, and programs that make using your tablet more productive.

Icons Used in This Book

 This icon flags useful, helpful tips or shortcuts.

This icon marks a friendly reminder to do something.

 This icon marks a friendly reminder not to do something.

 This icon alerts you to overly nerdy information and technical discussions of the topic at hand. Reading the information is optional, though it may win you the Daily Double on *Jeopardy!*

Beyond the Book

I didn't write this heading. The publisher did. It's a long story, but soon, the publisher will go back to publishing books and not giving away my stuff free on the Internet.

Bonus information for this title can be found online. You can visit the publisher's website to find an online cheat sheet at

`www.dummies.com/cheatsheet/samsunggalaxytabs`

Supplemental online material has been created for this book. Doesn't that make you feel better? And here you thought you paid for the entire book when you opened the cover. Oops! Now you have homework: Supplemental stuff can be found at

`www.dummies.com/extras/samsunggalaxytabs`

Updates to this book might someday be found at

`www.dummies.com/extras/samsunggalaxytabs`

I also do my own updates, blog posts, alerts, and helpful information, which is also free but far more engaging. My stuff is updated more frequently than the publisher's website because (last time I checked) I'm not a big corporation. You can find my own information at

`www.wambooli.com`

Specific support for the Galaxy Tab is found here:

`www.wambooli.com/help/galaxytabs/`

My email address is dgookin@wambooli.com. Yes, that's my real address. I reply to all email I get, and you'll get a quick reply if you keep your question short and specific to this book. Although I do enjoy saying "Hi," I cannot answer technical support questions, resolve billing issues, or help you troubleshoot your Galaxy Tab. Thanks for understanding.

Enjoy this book and your Galactic tablet!

Where to Go from Here

Hey! Thanks for hanging in there. Now I fully expect you to read the entire book, cover to cover, including the loopy ads at the end. *Chihuahuas For Dummies*? Are they serious?

Back to the topic at hand: Start reading! Observe the table of contents and find something that interests you. Or look up your puzzle in the index. When these suggestions don't cut it, just start reading Chapter 1.

Part I
A Galaxy in Your Hands

getting started
with

the Galaxy Tab

In this part. . .

⮞ Get started with your Samsung Galaxy Tab.

⮞ Work through the Tab setup.

⮞ Learn how to operate the tablet.

⮞ Discover various parts of a Galaxy Tab.

A Galactic Orientation

In This Chapter

▶ Unboxing your Galaxy tablet

▶ Charging the battery

▶ Locating important things

▶ Adding or removing a microSD card

▶ Getting optional accessories

▶ Storing the tablet

I thoroughly enjoy getting a new gizmo and opening its box. Expectations build. Joy is released. Then despair descends like a grand piano pushed out a third-story window. That's because any new electronic device, especially something as sophisticated as the Samsung Galaxy Tab, can be frustrating and confusing. You have a lot of ground to cover, so to make your journey easier, I offer this gentle introduction.

Set Up Your Galaxy Tablet

Most Galaxy tablets patiently wait in their box for your attention. The exception is the cellular, or LTE, tablet. Because it uses the mobile data signal, the kind people at the Phone Store might have worked through a setup and configuration process with you. This step is necessary to get the mobile data signal up and running. For non-cellular, or Wi-Fi only tablets, the initial configuration is left up to you.

Don't be frightened!

> ↙ Chapter 2 covers how the setup process works. Also discussed are the basic on-off operations for your tablet.

> ↙ An LTE tablet is one that uses the mobile data network to access the Internet. It can also use the Wi-Fi network. Yes, you pay monthly for that service.

✔ A Wi-Fi-only tablet uses only a Wi-Fi network for Internet access.

    ✔ The initial setup of an LTE tablet identifies the device with the cellular network, giving it a network ID and associating the ID with your cellular bill.

    ✔ Although a Wi-Fi tablet doesn't require setup with a cellular provider, it does require a Wi-Fi signal to access the Internet. Accessing that signal is a necessary step. See Chapter 16 for information on configuring your tablet for use with a Wi-Fi network.

Opening the box

Liberate your Galaxy Tab from its box by locating and lifting the cardboard tab. Gleefully remove any plastic sheeting that clings to the device. Check the sides, edges, front, and back. Also check the rear camera lens to ensure that it's not covered with plastic.

In the box's bottom compartment, you may find

    ✔ **A USB cable:** You can use it to connect the tablet to a computer or a wall charger.

    ✔ **A wall charger:** You'll find a USB connector (hole) on the charger, as well as metal prongs for plugging the thing into a wall socket.

    ✔ **Pamphlets with warnings and warranty information:** I find it amazing that the *Getting Started* pamphlet is about 2 percent of the size of the warnings and warranty information. I blame the discrepancy on lawyers, who are obviously better than technology writers at getting work.

    ✔ **Cover or pouch:** You may find a half cover for your Tab S inside the box. See the later section, "Attaching the cover." The Tab 4 might come with a special pouch into which you can tuck the tablet.

    ✔ **The 4G SIM card holder:** For the LTE/cellular tablet, you'll need a 4G SIM card. The Phone Store people may have tossed its holder into the box as well. You can throw it out.

    ✔ **Jimmy Hoffa:** The former labor leader disappeared in 1975, and no one has been able to find him. Look in the bottom of the box to see whether Hoffa's body is there. You never know.

Go ahead and free the USB cable and power charger from their clear plastic cocoons. That's because the next step is to charge the tablet's battery, covered in the following section.

Keep the box for as long as you own your tablet. If you ever need to return the device or ship it somewhere, the original box is the ideal container. You can shove the useless pamphlets and papers back into the box as well.

Charging the battery

The first thing that I recommend you do with your Galaxy Tab is to give it a full charge. Obey these steps:

1. **Plug one end of the USB cable into the wall adapter.**

2. **Attach the other end of the USB cable to the tablet.**

   The cable attaches to the tablet's edge: the right edge for horizontal tablets and the bottom edge for vertical tablets. The USB connector (hole) cannot be mistaken and the cable plugs in only one way.

3. **Plug the wall adapter into the wall.**

Upon success, you may see a Battery icon on the tablet's touchscreen. The icon gives you an idea of the current battery-power level and lets you know that the tablet is functioning properly. Don't be alarmed if the Battery icon fails to appear.

If the Welcome screen appears when you charge the tablet, you can proceed with the initial configuration, which is covered in Chapter 2. Or you can wait and finish reading this chapter first. Or have a cookie. It's always fun to ignore responsibility and have a cookie.

- ✔ Most tablets come partially charged from the factory. That's no excuse! I recommend giving your tablet a good initial charge. It also helps you become familiar with the process.

- ✔ The USB cable can also be used to connect the Galaxy Tab to a computer. See Chapter 17 for details.

- ✔ The tablet's battery also charges when the tablet is plugged into a computer's USB port, although it's not as effective as charging by using a wall socket.

- ✔ The Galaxy Tab does not have a removable, and therefore replaceable, battery.

Attaching the cover

If your Galaxy Tab S came with a half-cover, you can attach it to the device. If your Tab S didn't come with a cover, Samsung has suddenly gotten cheap and there's no excuse for such an omission.

The key to attaching the cover is to look for the two "buttons" on the back of the tablet. Originally, pressing those buttons caused the tablet to explode in an orange fireball of death. Then Samsung changed its mind, and now the buttons are designed to receive the snaps on the half-cover, to firmly attach the cover to the device.

Position the snaps on the shorter side of the half cover over the two buttons on the back of the Tab S. Press firmly. Snap. Snap. You're done.

Know Your Way around the Galaxy

"Second star to the right and straight on till morning" may get Peter Pan to Neverland, but you need more specific directions for navigating your way around your Galaxy Tab.

Finding things on the tablet

Many interesting and useful items festoon the front, back, and perimeter of your Galaxy Tab. Before going into detail, I must address the issue of which way is up on your tablet.

Generally speaking, the tablet's bottom edge features the Home button, illustrated in Figure 1-1. When I write about the tablet's top and bottom edges or its left and right edges, the orientation is set by the Home button's location. When you rotate the tablet, changing between horizontal and vertical orientations, the Home button is still "on the bottom."

Recent   Home   Back

Figure 1-1: Galaxy tablet navigation buttons.

Now that I've clarified which way is up, take a moment to peruse the following list and locate the items mentioned on your tablet.

Touchscreen display: The biggest part of the tablet is its touchscreen display, which occupies almost all the territory on the front of the device. The touchscreen display is a see-touch thing: You look at it and also touch it with your fingers to control the tablet. See Chapter 3 for details on touchscreen manipulation.

Navigation buttons: Found at the bottom center of the tablet, these buttons serve many key functions in the Android operating system. They are, as illustrated in Figure 1-1, Recent, Home, and Back. The Home button is a physical button. Recent and Back are touch-sensitive buttons. The functions of these buttons are covered in Chapter 3.

Front camera: The tablet's front-facing camera is centered above the touchscreen. The camera is used for taking self-portraits as well as for video chats. See Chapter 11 for information on using your Galaxy Tab as a camera; Chapter 7 covers video chat.

Light sensor: Just next to the front camera is a teensy light sensor. It's used to help adjust the brightness level of the touchscreen. It is not a second camera.

Power/USB connector: The Power/USB jack is located on the tablet's edge. For horizontal tablets, the connector is found on the right edge. For vertical tablets, the connector is found on the bottom. This location is where you attach the USB cable to the tablet.

Power Lock button: The Power Lock button is the smaller of two thin buttons on the edge of the device. Press Power Lock to turn on the tablet, to lock it (put it to sleep), to wake it up, and to turn it off. Directions for performing these tasks are found in Chapter 2.

Volume button: The tablet's volume button is the longer of the two buttons found on the device's edge. Press one side of the button to set the volume higher, and press the other side to set the volume lower. This button is found next to the Power Lock button.

Headphone jack: The tablet's largest hole accommodates a standard headphone plug. This is where you connect headphones to the tablet.

SIM card cover: This spot is used to access an LTE tablet's SIM card, and it's found only on LTE tablets. You do not need to open this cover or replace the SIM card unless you're switching cellular providers.

Media card slot: Lift the cover on this slot to add or remove a microSD memory card. See the next section.

IR Blaster: This port has a great name but a rather mundane function. It's a thin black rectangle found on the tablet's edge and it tastes like licorice. The IR Blaster sends an infrared signal to another device, such as a TV. It's used primarily with the WatchOn app, covered in Chapter 23.

Speaker(s): Stereo speakers are located on opposite edges on the tablet, although smaller tablets put the speakers on the back.

Microphone: A tiny hole on the tablet serves as the device's microphone. The hole's location may not be apparent — it's about the diameter of a pinhead — but it's there. Avoid the temptation to stick anything into that wee li'l hole.

Rear camera and flash: The rear camera is found on the back of the tablet. If your Galaxy Tab camera features a flash, the flash LED is found nearby the camera.

✔ Be careful not to confuse the SIM card with the removable storage media (microSD) card. They're not the same thing. You'll rarely, if ever, access the SIM card.

✔ SIM stands for Subscriber Identity Module. The SIM card is used by your cellular provider to identify your tablet and keep track of the amount of data it accesses. Yep, that's so you can be billed properly. The SIM also gives your cellular tablet a phone number, though that's merely an account number and not something you can dial or send a text message to.

Inserting and removing a microSD card

Expand your tablet's storage capacity by installing a microSD card. The card stores photos, music, and other information, supplementing the tablet's internal storage. You can use the card also to exchange files between the tablet and other devices, such as a computer.

The microSD card can be inserted whether the device is on or off. Heed these directions:

1. **Locate the microSD card hatch on the tablet's edge.**

   Figure 1-2 illustrates the hatch's appearance, although it may look subtly different on your tablet. The hatch is labeled *microSD*; don't confuse it with the SIM card cover.

   Lift here

2. **Insert a fingernail into the slot on the teensy hatch that covers the microSD slot, and then flip up the hatch.**

   Figure 1-2: Opening the memory card hatch.

   The slot cover has a fingernail-size indentation, similar to what's shown in Figure 1-2. When pressure is applied, the hatch that covers the slot pops up and kind of flops over to the side. The slot cover doesn't come off completely.

3. **Orient the microSD card so that the printed side is up and the teeny triangle on the card is pointing toward the open slot.**

4. **Use your fingernail or a bent paperclip to gently shove the card all the way into the slot.**

   The card makes a faint clicking sound when it's fully inserted.

   If the card keeps popping out, you're not shoving it in far enough.

5. **Close the hatch covering the microSD card slot.**

If the tablet is on (and has been configured), you may see a prompt informing you that the card has been inserted.

To remove the microSD card, follow these steps:

1. **If the tablet is on, unmount the microSD card. If the tablet is off, skip to Step 2.**

   Before you attempt this process, reading Chapters 2 and 3 helps.

   a. *At the Home screen, touch the Apps icon to visit the Apps screen.*

   b. *Open the Settings app.*

   c. *Tap the General tab atop the screen; then on the left side of the screen, choose the Storage category.*

  d. *Under the SD Card heading on the right side of the screen, choose Unmount SD Card.*

  e. *Ignore the warning, and then touch the OK button.*

A message appears briefly atop the touchscreen, telling you that it's okay to remove the microSD card; proceed with Step 2.

2. **Open the little hatch covering the microSD card slot.**

3. **Using your fingernail or a bent paperclip, push the microSD card inward a tad.**

The microSD slot is spring-loaded, so pressing in the card pops it outward.

4. **Pinch the microSD card between your fingers and remove it completely.**

When the tablet is turned off, you can insert or remove the microSD card at will. Refer to Chapter 2 for information on turning off your Galaxy tablet.

✔ You cannot unmount the microSD card when the tablet is connected to a computer. Disconnect the tablet and try again.

✔ Odds are good that your tablet didn't come with a microSD card, so run out and buy one!

✔ The microSD cards arc tccnsy. To usc thc card on a computer or another electronic device, get an SD card adapter.

✔ The Galaxy Tab S accepts microSD cards up to 128GB in capacity. You'll find less expensive microSD cards in capacities of 16GB, 32GB, and 64GB.

✔ GB is an abbreviation for *gigabyte,* which is one billion characters of storage. One gigabyte is enough storage for about an hour of video, or a week's worth of music, or a year's worth of photographs. It's a lot of storage.

✔ SD stands for *Secure Digital*. It is but one of about a zillion different media card standards.

✔ The tablet works with or without a microSD card installed.

✔ Refer to Chapter 17 for more information on storage.

Getting optional accessories

As this book goes to press, the only official Galaxy Tab accessories available are special covers or jackets. You might want to look into several unofficial accessories as well. Here's what I recommend:

Earphones: You can use earphones from any standard smartphone or portable media player with your tablet. Simply plug the earphones into the tablet's headphone jack and you're ready to go.

Bluetooth keyboard: Your Galaxy Tab works with any Bluetooth keyboard, which gives you the option of using a real keyboard with the device. Even keyboards for those i-fruit company tablets work with your tablet.

Vehicle charger: You can charge the tablet while in your car by using a vehicle charger. This adapter plugs into the car's 12-volt power supply, in the receptacle once known as the cigarette lighter. The vehicle charger is a must-have if you plan to use the Galaxy tablet navigation features in your auto or you need a charge on the road.

Additional accessories may be available. Check the location where your Tab was sold to inquire about new items.

✔ None of this extra stuff is essential to using the tablet.

✔ If the earphones feature a microphone, you can use the microphone for dictation and audio recording on the tablet.

✔ If the earphones feature a button, you can use the button to pause and play music. Press the button once to pause and again to play.

✔ See Chapter 16 for more information on pairing your tablet with a Bluetooth keyboard.

Where to Keep Your Tab

Like your car keys, glasses, wallet, and light saber, you'll want to keep your Galaxy tablet in a place where it's safe, easy to find, and always handy whether you're at home, at work, on the road, or in a galaxy far, far away.

Making a home for the tablet

I recommend keeping your Galaxy Tab in the same spot when you've finished using it. My first suggestion is to make a place next to your computer. Keep the charging cord handy or just plug the cord into the computer's USB port so that you can synchronize information with your computer regularly and keep the tablet charged.

Another handy place to keep the tablet is on your nightstand. See Chapter 14 for information on using the tablet to satisfy your nighttime reading or video watching. It can also serve as an alarm clock.

Avoid keeping the tablet anyplace where it may get too hot. Avoid setting it on a windowsill, on a car dashboard, or anywhere in direct sunlight for prolonged periods of time.

Keep the tablet visible. Don't put it where someone might sit on it, step on it, or otherwise damage it. And don't leave the tablet under a stack of newspapers on a table or a counter, where it might get accidentally tossed out or recycled.

Never leave your tablet unattended on the planet Venus.

As long as you return the tablet to the same spot when you're done with it, you'll always know where it is.

Taking the tablet with you

If you're like me, you probably carry your Galactic tablet with you around the house, in the office, at the airport, in the air, or while you're in the car. I hope you're not using the tablet while you're driving! Regardless, have a portable place to store your tablet while you're on the road.

The ideal storage spot for the tablet is a specially designed Galaxy Tab carrying case or pouch, such as the type of pouches mama kangaroos have, but without the expense of owning a zoo. A case keeps the tablet from being dinged, scratched, or even unexpectedly turned on while it's in your back-pack, purse, carry-on luggage, or wherever you put the tablet when you aren't using it.

Also see Chapter 21 for information on using your Galaxy Tab on the road.

The On and Off Chapter

*I*n the book *Lamps For Dummies*, the chapter for turning a lamp on or off is barely a page long. That's because lamps haven't changed much in the past 100 years; they still have two modes, on and off. You would think that turning a Galaxy Tab on and off would require similar brevity. Alas, that's not the case.

For starters, your tablet lacks an on-off switch. Instead, it offers a Power Lock button, which serves multiple functions. Next, multiple options are available for dismissing the tablet. Unlike turning off a lamp, you can turn off, restart, or lock your tablet. These features, which are necessary for a sophisticated piece of technology, require that this chapter be more than a page long.

Hello, Tablet

Turning on the Galaxy Tab is fairly simple: Press and hold down the Power Lock button. Eventually the touch-screen comes to life, impressing you with Samsung's startup graphics and sound. Short. Sweet. Simple.

Sadly, there's more to the story than short, sweet, and simple.

The tablet won't start unless the battery is charged. See Chapter 1.

Turning on your Galaxy tablet (for the first time)

The very, very first time your Galaxy tablet is turned on is a special event. That's when you configure the device, answering various questions and setting a few basic options. After this ordeal, turning on the tablet is fast and easy; see the next section, "Turning on your tablet."

The initial setup involves several steps, which may change after this book goes to press. I recommend reading over the following list to familiarize yourself with the process. Then use the steps as a reference if you need assistance.

1. **Turn on the tablet by pressing the Power Lock button.**

   You may have to press the button longer than you think; when the tablet's logo appears on the screen, the tablet has started.

   It's okay to turn on the tablet while it's plugged in and charging.

2. **Choose your language.**

   Yes, if you're reading this in English, you choose English as the language for your tablet.

3. **Activate the cellular tablet.**

   This step was most likely done at the Phone Store. If it wasn't, follow the directions on the screen and wait for the connection to be established.

   Choose an available Wi-Fi network from the list. Type the password. Tap the Connect button. More detailed steps are provided in Chapter 16.

   Even if you have a cellular Galaxy Tab, connect to a Wi-Fi network, if one is available. Using Wi-Fi incurs no fees, unlike the mobile data connection.

4. **Confirm that the date and time are correct.**

   If not, touch the screen to set the date and time. I recommend setting the time zone before you set the time.

5. **Agree to the terms and conditions.**

   Touch the box to place or remove the check mark. I recommend activating the tablet's location features, which helps with navigation. See Chapter 10.

   You do not need to submit troubleshooting information to Samsung.

6. **Sign into your Google account.**

   You can always associate your Google account later, but get it out of the way now. If you don't have a Google account, sign up for one. See the section, "More Accounts for Your Tab."

7. **Personalize your account.**

   Type your first and last name, unless they were already supplied magically.

8. **If you have a Samsung or Dropbox account, log in when prompted.**

   You don't need to sign up for a Samsung or Dropbox account if you don't want to; feel free to skip this step.

9. **Tap the Finish button when setup is complete.**

   You can now use your tablet.

The good news is that you're done. Setup is a process you endure only once on the Galaxy Tab. From this point on, starting the tablet works as described in the next few sections.

Except: You may have to endure a cavalcade of updates after starting your tablet for the very first time. Proceed with installing any given updates. I recommend keeping the tablet plugged in. Obey the prompts on the screen.

Don't be surprised when you see multiple updates. This happens a lot when you first activate an Android tablet.

Who is this Android person?

Just like a computer, your Samsung tablet has an operating system. It's the main program in charge of all the software, or apps, inside the tablet. Unlike on a computer, however, Android is a mobile device operating system, designed primarily for use in tablets and smartphones.

Android is based on the Linux operating system, which is also a computer operating system. Linux is much more stable and bug-free than Windows, so it's not as popular. Google owns, maintains, and develops Android, which is why your online Google information is synced with the Galaxy Tab. The Android mascot, shown here, often appears on Android apps or hardware. He has no official name, though most folks call him Andy.

✔ Most of the settings, choices, and options you've made during the initial setup process can be changed later. For example, you can connect with another Wi-Fi network, add another Google Account, or enable or disable location settings.

✔ See Chapter 15 for information on obtaining apps from the Google Play Store.

✔ See the sidebar "Who is this Android person?" for more information about the Android operating system.

Turning on your tablet

To turn on your Galaxy tablet, press and hold down the Power Lock button. After a few seconds, you see the tablet's start-up logo and then some hypnotic animation. The tablet is coming to life.

Eventually, you see the unlock screen. See the section "Working the Lock screen" for details on what to do next.

Unlocking the tablet

It's natural for your Galaxy Tab to be on and locked. The device is working, but the touchscreen is off, similar to a computer operating in sleep mode. The tablet operates this way when you're not actively using it. Its battery supports keeping the device on and locked for lengthy periods of time.

Choose any of these techniques to unlock the tablet:

✔ Press the Power Lock button. Unlike when turning on the tablet, a quick press is all that's needed.

✔ Press the Home button.

✔ Open the half cover on the Tab S, if it's installed.

✔ Connect or disconnect the USB cable (when the cable is supplying power).

After unlocking the tablet, you see the Lock screen. Work the screen lock as described in the next section, and then you can start using the device.

The tablet automatically locks when it's bored or after you ignored it for a while. While locked, the touchscreen turns off to save power. See the section "Locking the tablet," later in this chapter, for information on how to manually lock the tablet.

Working the Lock screen

The Galaxy Tab has six locks for its Lock screen. These locks provide extra security, although most of the locks aren't considered that secure. Here are the available locks:

Swipe: The standard screen lock. Swipe your finger on the screen to unlock the device, as illustrated in Figure 2-1.

Pattern: Trace a preset pattern over the nine dots on the screen.

Fingerprint: Rub your finger or thumb over the Home button to unlock the device. This screen lock is available only the Galaxy Tab S.

PIN: Type a number to unlock the device.

Password: Type a password, which can include letters, numbers, and symbols.

None: The device features no Lock screen; you can use the tablet immediately.

One of these locks appears when you turn on or unlock the tablet. Or in the case of the None setting, no lock appears.

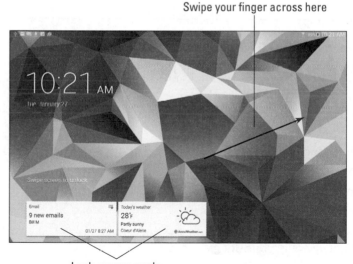

Figure 2-1: The basic unlocking screen.

- ✔ The most secure locks are PIN and Password. The Pattern and Fingerprint are moderately secure, although not foolproof. The None and Swipe settings are not considered secure.

- ✔ When the Swipe lock is enabled, you may see some startup app icons on the Lock screen. Swipe an icon by dragging it with your finger, and that app starts.

- ✔ The Lock screen won't appear when the None screen lock is chosen.

- ✔ The PIN and Password locks are required for certain tablet security settings, such as when you have a kid's account configured or you use the tablet to access a secure email system.

- ✔ Screen locks are configured by using the Settings app. Refer to Chapter 20 for details.

More Accounts for Your Tab

The Galaxy Tab can be home to your various online incarnations, including your email accounts, online services, subscriptions, plus other digital personas. I recommend adding those accounts to your tablet to continue the setup and configuration process.

With the tablet on and unlocked, follow these steps:

1. **Touch the Apps icon.**

   The Apps icon is located on the Home screen (and shown in the margin).

2. **Open the Settings app.**

   You may have to swipe the Apps screen right or left to locate the Settings app.

   After touching the Settings icon, the Settings screen appears. It lists items for configuring and setting tablet options.

3. **Tap the General tab.**

4. **Select the Accounts category.**

   You see any existing accounts, as shown in Figure 2-2, although you might see only your Google account.

5. **Tap Add Account.**

Accounts item   General tab   Add account

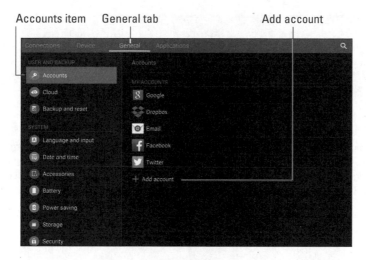

Figure 2-2: Accounts in the Settings app.

6. Select an account type from the list.

For example, if you haven't yet added your Google account, choose Google.

Don't worry if you don't see the exact type of account you want to add. You may have to add an app before a specific account appears. Chapter 15 covers adding apps.

7. Follow the directions on the screen to sign into your account.

Generally speaking, you sign in using an existing username and password. Some accounts may have an option that lets you create an account when you don't already have one.

You can continue adding accounts by repeating these steps. When you're done, press the Home button to return to the Home screen.

- See Chapter 6 for specific information on adding email accounts to your Galaxy Tab.

- Chapter 9 covers social networking on your tablet. Refer to that chapter for information on adding Facebook and Twitter accounts.

- The accounts you add are your own. If you need to add another user to the tablet (who would have her own accounts), see Chapter 20 for information.

Transferring information from your old tablet

Here's one task you don't need to worry about: All the Google information associated with your old tablet — your current phone — is instantly transferred to your Samsung Galaxy Tab. This information includes contacts, Gmail, events, and other Googly account data. You can even install apps you've previously obtained (free or purchased), although you need to do so manually. See Chapter 15.

As you add other accounts to your Tab, the information associated with those accounts is migrated as well. The only category not migrated is media installed on the other device. If you've synchronized the media with an online-sharing service, the information can easily be transferred. Otherwise, refer to Chapter 17 for information on moving over photos, videos, and music to your new Galaxy Tab.

Farewell, Tablet

I know of three ways to say goodbye to your Galaxy tablet, and only one of them involves a steamroller. The other methods are documented in this section.

Locking the tablet

To lock the tablet, simply press the Power Lock button. The touchscreen goes dark; the tablet is locked.

✒ The tablet continues to work while it's locked; it receives email, can play music, and signals alerts. While it's locked, the tablet doesn't use as much power as it would with the display on.

✒ Your tablet will spend most of its time locked.

✒ Locking doesn't turn off the tablet.

✒ Any timers or alarms you set still activate when the tablet is locked. See Chapter 14 for information on setting timers and alarms.

✒ To unlock the tablet, press and release the Power Lock button. See the section "Unlocking the tablet," earlier in this chapter.

✒ Refer to Chapter 19 for information on setting the automatic timeout value for the Lock screen.

Turning off your Galaxy Tab

To turn off the tablet, heed these steps:

1. **Press and hold down the Power Lock button.**

   You see the Device Options menu, shown in Figure 2-3.

   If you chicken out and don't want to turn off the tablet, touch the Back button to dismiss the Device Options menu.

2. **Choose the Power Off item.**

3. **Tap OK.**

   The tablet turns itself off.

Figure 2-3: The Device Options menu.

The tablet doesn't run when it's off, so it doesn't remind you of appointments, collect email, or let you hear any alarms you've set.

The tablet also isn't angry with you for turning it off, though you may sense some resentment when you turn it on again.

- ✔ The Vibrate option, shown in Figure 2-3, doesn't appear on tablets that lack that feature.

- ✔ Keep the tablet in a safe place while it's turned off. Refer to Chapter 1 for storage suggestions.

Restarting the tablet

When you must turn the tablet off and then turn it on again, choose Restart from the Device Options menu. (Refer to Figure 2-3.) A restart often fixes minor tablet woes.

- ✔ You'll rarely need to restart the Galaxy Tab.

- ✔ See Chapter 22 for information on tablet troubleshooting.

How Your Galaxy Tab Works

In This Chapter

▶ Working the touchscreen

▶ Changing the volume

▶ Understanding the Home screen

▶ Checking notifications

▶ Running apps

▶ Multitasking

▶ Identifying various icons

A t one time, you could gauge how advanced a piece of technology was by how many buttons it had. Early computers with their dozens of switches and blinking lights represented the pinnacle of twentieth-century achievement. Then things began to change.

Today's most advanced technology, which is the Galaxy tablet you hold in your hands, sports few buttons and only one blinking light. The absence of buttons and blinking lights means that you must control the device in other ways.

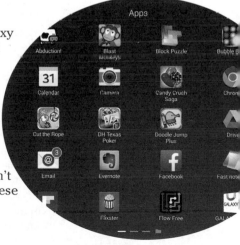

Basic Operations

The Galaxy Tab can intimidate you only when you don't understand a few basic things about how it works. These items generally involve the touchscreen, which is the tablet's main interface with a human being.

Touching the touchscreen

To control your Galaxy Tab, you need to touch the screen. You can use one or two fingers, or you could use the tip of your big toe sticking out of your sock. It doesn't matter how, but touch the screen you must.

Here are some of the common ways to manipulate the touchscreen:

Tap: The basic touchscreen maneuver is to touch it. You tap an object, an icon, a control, a menu item, a doodad, and so on. The tap operation is similar to a mouse click on a computer. It may also be referred to as a *touch* or a *press*.

Double-tap: Touch the screen twice in the same location. Double-tapping can be used to zoom in on an image or a map, but it can also zoom out. Because of the double-tap's dual nature, I recommend instead using the pinch or spread operation to zoom.

Long-press: Touch part of the screen and keep down your finger. Depending on what you're doing, a pop-up menu may appear, or the item you're long-pressing may get "picked up" so that you can move it around. A long-press might also be referred to as *touch and hold down* in some documentation.

Swipe: To swipe, you touch your finger on one spot and then move your finger to another spot. Swipes can go up, down, left, or right; the touchscreen content moves in the direction in which you swipe your finger. A swipe can be fast or slow. It's also called a *flick* or a *slide*.

Drag: A combination of long-press and then swipe, the drag operation moves items on the screen.

Pinch: A pinch involves two fingers, which start out separated and then are brought together. The effect is used to *zoom out,* to reduce the size of an image or see more of a map.

Spread: The opposite of pinch is spread. You start out with your fingers together and then spread them. The spread is used to *zoom in,* to enlarge an image or see more detail on a map.

Rotate: A few apps let you rotate an image on the screen by touching with two fingers and twisting them around a center point. Think of turning a combination lock on a safe to best understand the rotate operation.

You can't manipulate the touchscreen while wearing gloves unless they're gloves designed for using electronic touchscreens, such as the gloves that Batman wears.

Changing the orientation

Your Galaxy Tab features a gizmo called an *accelerometer,* which determines in which direction the tablet is pointed or whether you've reoriented the device from an upright to a horizontal position, or even upside down. That way, the information on the touchscreen always appears upright, no matter how you hold the Tab.

To demonstrate how the tablet orients itself, rotate the device clockwise or counterclockwise. Most apps change their orientation to match however you've turned the tablet (see Figure 3-1).

Vertical orientation   Horizontal orientation

Figure 3-1: Galaxy tablet orientation.

The rotation feature may not work for all apps, especially games, which may present themselves in one orientation only.

- ✔ The onscreen keyboard is more usable when the tablet is in its horizontal orientation. See Chapter 4.

- ✔ You can lock the orientation if the rotating screen bothers you. See the "Making quick settings" section, later in this chapter.

- ✔ A nifty application for demonstrating the accelerometer is the game Labyrinth. It can be purchased at the Google Play Store, or the free version, Labyrinth Lite, can be downloaded. See Chapter 15 for more information about the Google Play Store.

Using the navigation buttons

Below the touchscreen dwell three buttons. The middle one is a real button you press; the outside two are touch-sensitive buttons. These are the navigation buttons, and they help get you around as you use your Galaxy tablet.

Home: No matter what you're doing on the tablet, pressing this button displays the Home screen. When you're already viewing the Home screen, touching the Home button returns you to the main Home screen. See the later section, "Behold the Home Screens."

Back: The Back button serves several purposes, all of which fit neatly under the concept of "back." Press the button to return to a previous page, dismiss an onscreen menu, close a window, hide the onscreen keyboard, and so on.

Recent: Touching the Recent button displays the Overview. See the later section, "Switching between running apps," for details.

Setting the volume

Sometimes the sound level is too loud. Sometimes it's too soft. And rarely, it's just right. Finding that just-right level is the job of the Volume key that clings to the edge of your Galaxy tablet.

If the Volume key is on top of your tablet, press the left part of the key to increase the volume and the right part to decrease the volume. If the Volume key is on the side of your tablet, press the top part to make the volume louder and the bottom part to make the volume softer.

As you press the Volume key, a graphic appears on the touchscreen to illustrate the relative volume level, as shown in Figure 3-2.

Tap the Settings icon, shown in Figure 3-2, to see detailed volume controls. You can individually set the volume for notifications, media, and system sounds, as shown in the expanded onscreen volume control: Swipe the white dot left or right to set the volume.

> ✏ Notifications are alerts to new items, such as incoming email, a chat request, or an appointment reminder.

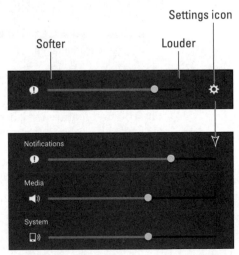

Figure 3-2: Setting the volume.

- Media includes music that plays, sound from a video, and noise in a video game.

- System sounds are the noise made by the onscreen keyboard, warnings, alarms, and similar audio.

- When the volume is set all the way down, the tablet is silenced and placed in vibration mode. (Not every tablet features vibration mode.)

- Sound can also be adjusted by using the Sound Quick Action. See the later section, "Making quick settings."

- The Settings app is the primary location for setting sounds. Refer to Chapter 19 for details.

- The Volume key works even when the tablet is locked. That means you don't need to unlock the device to adjust the volume when you're listening to music.

Behold the Home Screens

The main base from which you begin exploration of your Galaxy Tab is the *Home* screen. It's the first thing you see after unlocking the tablet, and the place you go to whenever you quit an app.

To view the Home screen at any time, press the Home button, which is found on the front of the tablet, right below the touchscreen.

Switching between Classic and Content Home screens

The Galaxy Tab S features two sets of Home screens. The traditional Home screen is available and is called the Classic Home screen. An alternative Home screen is also available. It's called the Content Home screen. Both Home screens are shown in Figure 3-3.

On the Tab S, you switch to the Content Home screen by swiping the Classic Home screen from left to right. When the screen fills with widget tiles, you're viewing the Content Home screen.

To switch to the Classic Home screen, swipe the Content Home screen right to left. An index at the bottom of the screen shows which Home screen you're viewing, as illustrated in Figure 3-4.

Each Home screen, Classic and Content, holds several pages, like a street of Home screens. Swipe the screen left or right to flip between the pages.

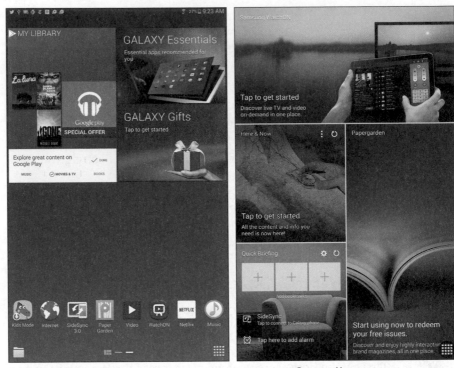

Classic Home screen   Content Home screen

Figure 3-3: Classic and Content Home screens.

When you press the Home button, you're returned to the last Home screen page you viewed on either the Classic or Content Home screen. Each Home screen features a main page. When you press the Home key a second time, you're shown the main page.

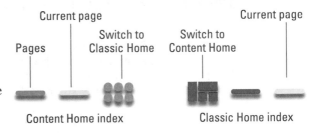

Figure 3-4: The Home screen index.

This book's focus is primarily on the Classic Home screen, which is referred to as the *Home screen* in the text. The Classic Home screen is always mentioned as such.

➤ The Galaxy Tab 4 uses only the Classic Home screen. A house icon appears on the Home screen index, which identifies the main Home screen page.

✔ Feel free to ignore the Content Home screen. It's unique to the Galaxy Tab S. My observation is that Samsung makes additions like this for one of device and then drops it from the next edition.

✔ The biggest difference between the Classic and Content Home screens? Icons! The Classic Home screen features app launcher icons in addition to widgets. The Content Home screen shows only widgets.

✔ See Chapter 19 for information on managing the Home screen pages, adding new ones, and setting which page is the main one.

Touring the Home screen

Many interesting items festoon the Home screen, known as the Classic Home screen on the Galaxy Tab S. These items are illustrated in Figure 3-5.

I recommend that you familiarize yourself with the following items and terms when using the Home screen:

Status bar: The top part of the screen, this area shows notification icons and status icons. The status bar may disappear, in which case a quick swipe of the screen from the top downward will redisplay it.

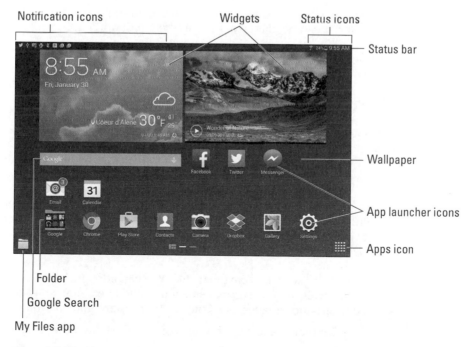

Figure 3-5: The Home screen.

Notification icons: These icons come and go, depending on what happens in your digital life. Notification icons appear whenever you receive a new email message or have a pending appointment. The next section, "Reviewing notifications," describes how to deal with notifications.

Status icons: These icons represent the tablet's current condition, such as the type of network it's connected to, its signal strength, and its battery status, as well as whether the tablet is connected to a Wi-Fi network or using Bluetooth, for example.

App launcher icons: The meat of the meal on the Home screen plate, app (application) launcher icons are where the action takes place. Touching a launcher icon opens an app.

Widgets: A widget is a window through which you view information, control the tablet, access features, or do something purely amusing. A special widget is the Google Search widget, which lets you search the Internet or use the powerful Google Now feature.

Folders: Multiple apps can be stored in a folder. Touch the folder to see a pop-up window that lists all the apps. Touch an app icon to start. See Chapter 18 for more information on folders.

Wallpaper: The background image you see on the Home screen is the wallpaper. It can be changed, as described in Chapter 19.

My Files app: This icon provides quick access to the My Files app on the Galaxy Tab S. It appears in the bottom-left corner of every Classic Home screen page. See Chapter 17 for information on using that app, which is available also on the Tab 4, just not pasted to the Home screen.

Apps icon: Touch the Apps icon to display the Apps screen, where all the apps installed on your tablet are found. This icon appears in the lower-right corner of every Home screen page, both for the Classic and Content Home screens. See the later section "Visiting the Apps screen" for details.

Ensure that you recognize the names of the various parts of the Home screen. These terms are used throughout this book and in whatever other scant Galaxy Tab documentation exists. Directions for using the Home screen gizmos are found throughout this chapter.

✔ The Home screen is customizable. You can add and remove icons, widgets, folders, and shortcuts, and even change wallpaper (background) images. See Chapter 19 for more information.

✔ The Content Home screen shows only widgets and the Apps icon.

 ✔ You may see numbers affixed to some Home screen icons. These numbers indicate pending actions, such as the unread email messages indicated by the icon shown in the margin.

Reviewing notifications

Notifications appear as icons at the top left of the Home screen (refer to Figure 3-5). To review the lot, pull down the notifications shade by swiping the screen from the tippy-top downward. The notifications panel is illustrated in Figure 3-6.

Touch a notification to deal with it. What happens next depends on the notification, but most often the app that generated the notification appears. You might also be given the opportunity to deal with whatever caused the notification, such as a calendar appointment.

Dismiss an individual notification by swiping to the right or left. To dismiss all notifications, tap the X (delete) icon. Some ongoing notifications, such as the USB notification in Figure 3-6, cannot be dismissed.

When you're finished looking, you can slide the notifications shade up again: Swipe the notifications shade handle by dragging your finger up the screen. If you find this process frustrating (and it is), press the Back button.

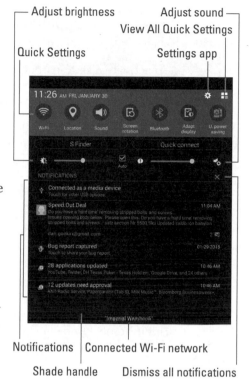

Figure 3-6: The notifications panel.

- While you can view notification icons when the tablet is locked, you cannot view the notifications panel.

- Notification icons disappear after their notification item has been dealt with.

- Dismissing some notifications doesn't prevent them from appearing again in the future. For example, notifications to update your programs continue to appear, as do calendar reminders.

- Some apps, such as Facebook and Twitter, don't display notifications unless you're logged in. See Chapter 9.

- The tablet plays a notification ringtone when a new notification floats in. See Chapter 19 for information on choosing which sound plays.

Making quick settings

Many common settings and features for your Galaxy Tab can be found atop the notifications panel. These Quick Settings appear as large icons (refer to Figure 3-6).

To activate a setting, touch its icon. When the setting is on, it appears highlighted in green. Tap a highlighted setting to turn it off. For example, tap the Sound Quick Setting to instantly mute the tablet.

Swipe the Quick Settings left or right to view more icons. Tap the View All icon (refer to Figure 3-6) to see all available Quick Settings.

Various Quick Settings are covered throughout this book. Generally speaking, any tablet feature that can be turned on or off — such as Wi-Fi, Bluetooth, Airplane mode, Sound, and so on — can be accessed quickly from a Quick Settings icon.

All About Those Apps

The primary thing you do on the Classic Home screen is run apps. That's made possible thanks to the app launcher icons that appear on the Classic Home screen. Knowing how to start, or launch, an app is key to getting the most from your Galaxy Tab.

- ✔ App is short for *application*. It's another word for *program* or *software*.
- ✔ Also see Chapter 23 for information on running apps by using the Multi Window feature.

Starting an app

To start an app, tap its icon. The app starts.

Apps can be started from the Classic Home screen: Tap a launcher icon to start the associated app. Apps can be started also from the Apps screen, as described in the next section.

You can also start an app found in a Home screen folder: Tap to open the folder, then tap an icon to start that app.

Quitting an app

Unlike a computer, you don't need to quit apps on your Galaxy Tab. To leave an app, press the Home button to return to the Home screen. You can keep pressing the Back button to back out of an app. Or you can press the Recent button to switch to another running app.

- ✒ A handful of apps feature a Quit or Exit command, but for the most part you don't quit an app on your tablet.

- ✒ If necessary, the Android operating system shuts down apps you haven't used in a while. You can directly stop apps running amok, as described in Chapter 18.

Visiting the Apps screen

The launcher icons you see on the Home screen don't represent all the apps in your tablet. To view all installed apps, you must visit the Apps screen: Tap the Apps icon on the Home screen. You see the first page of the Apps screen, as shown in Figure 3-7.

Similar to the Home screen, the Apps screen has several pages of apps. An index appears at the bottom of the screen (refer to Figure 3-7). Swipe the screen left or right to view the various pages.

To start an app from the Apps screen, tap its icon. The app starts.

The far right Apps screen page contains app folders, similar to the app folders found on the Home screen. You can use the folders to help organize your apps.

Open a folder by tapping its icon. Then tap an app icon to start that app.

- ✒ Consider placing launcher icons on the Home screen for those apps you use most often. See Chapter 18.

- ✒ See Chapter 18 also for information on creating Apps screen folders.

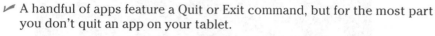

Wonderful widgets

Like apps, widgets appear on the Home screen, both Classic and Content versions. To use a widget, touch it. What happens after that depends on the widget and what it does.

For example, the YouTube widget lets you peruse videos. The Calendar widget shows a preview of your upcoming schedule. A Twitter widget may display recent tweets. Other widgets do interesting things, display useful information, or give you access to the tablet's settings or features.

See Chapter 18 for details on working with widgets on the Home screen.

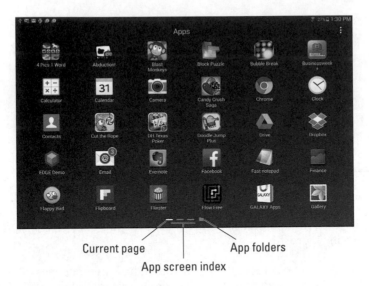

Current page

App folders

App screen index

Figure 3-7: The Apps screen.

Switching between running apps

The apps you run on your Galaxy Tab don't quit when you dismiss them from the screen. For the most part, they stay running. To switch between running apps, or to any app you've recently opened, press the Recent button, shown in the margin. You see the Overview on the screen, similar to what's shown in Figure 3-8.

Open Task Manager

Clear the list

Figure 3-8: Recently used apps on the Overview.

Choose an app from the Overview to switch to it.

✔ You can remove an app from the Overview by swiping it up or down (or left or right, when the tablet is held in a vertical orientation). This is almost the same thing as quitting an app. Almost.

✔ Clear the Overview by tapping the Close All icon.

✔ Task Manager provides another way to manage apps. See Chapter 23.

✔ Apps on your Galaxy Tab lack a quit or exit command. They keep running, so using the Overview is a great way to switch between running apps.

✔ Also remember that the Android operating system may shut down apps that haven't received attention for a while. Don't be surprised if you see an app missing from the Overview. If so, just start it up again as you normally would.

Recognizing common icons

In additional to the navigation icons, various other icons appear while you use your Galaxy Tab. These icons serve common functions in your apps as well as in the Android operating system. Table 3-1 lists the most common icons and their functions.

Table 3-1		Common Icons
Icon	*Name*	*Function*
◣	Action Bar	Displays a pop-up menu. This teensy icon appears in the lower-right corner of a button or an image, indicating that actions (commands) are attached.
⋮	Action Overflow	Displays a menu or a list of commands (actions).
＋	Add	Adds or creates a new item. The plus symbol (+) may be used with other symbols, depending on the app.
✕	Close	Closes a window or clears text from an input field.
🗑	Delete	Removes one or more items from a list or deletes a message.
✓	Done	Dismisses an action bar, such as the text-editing action bar.

(continued)

Table 3-1 *(continued)*

Icon	Name	Function
	Edit	Lets you edit an item, add text, or fill in fields.
	Dictation	Lets you use your voice to dictate text.
	Refresh	Fetches new information or reloads.
	Search	Search the tablet or the Internet for some tidbit of information.
	Settings	Adjusts options for an app.
	Share	Shares information stored on the tablet via email, social networking, or other Internet services.
	Favorite	Flags a favorite item, such as a contact or a web page.

Various sections throughout this book give examples of using the icons. Their images appear in the book's margins where relevant.

Other common symbols are used on icons in various apps. For example, the standard Play and Pause icons are used as well.

Text to Type and Edit

In This Chapter

▶ Using the onscreen keyboard

▶ Accessing special characters

▶ Creating text by using keyboard swipe

▶ Dictating text with voice input

▶ Editing text

▶ Selecting, cutting, copying, and pasting text

If a tablet had a keyboard, it would be a laptop, not a tablet. The notion of a keyboard adds too many buttons to an otherwise sleek and mobile device. Even so, text input is still required. While you most likely won't use your Galactic tablet to write a novel, you are required to write text. To fulfill that function, and to help you edit and hone your text, you use something called the onscreen keyboard.

This Is a Keyboard?

The onscreen keyboard reveals itself on the bottom half of the screen, like to the Galaxy Tab S keyboard shown in Figure 4-1. The Galaxy Tab 4 keyboard is similar, although it's missing the Del, Ctrl, and triangle keys.

In Figure 4-1, the onscreen keyboard is shown in alphabetic mode. You see keys from A through Z in lowercase, plus number and symbol keys, along with other keys for functions fun and frustrating.

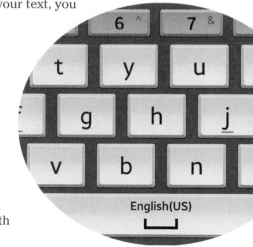

Figure 4-1: The onscreen keyboard.

The Enter key changes its look depending on what you're typing. Five variations are shown in Figure 4-1. Here's what each one does:

- **Enter:** Just like the Enter or Return key on a computer keyboard, this key ends a paragraph of text. It's used mostly when filling in long stretches of text or when multiline input is needed.

- **Go:** This action key directs an app to do something, such as visit a web page.

- **Search:** This key appears when you're searching for something. Tap the key to start the search.

- **Next:** This key appears when you're typing information in multiple fields. Touch this key to switch from one field to the next, such as when typing a username and a password.

- **Done:** This key appears when you've finished typing text in the final field and are ready to submit the information.

The large key at the bottom center of the onscreen keyboard is the Space key. To the right of the Space key on the Tab S are two triangle keys you touch to move the cursor, which helps you to edit text.

Some keys change, depending on what you're typing. For example, when entering a web page address, the Space key changes size to accommodate a slash key, a colon key, and a www key. These extra keys are useful when you type a web page address. Don't be surprised when the keyboard changes — and take advantage of those special keys when they appear.

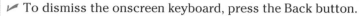

- To summon the onscreen keyboard, touch any text field or spot on the screen where typing is permitted.

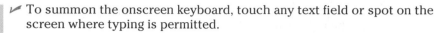

- To dismiss the onscreen keyboard, press the Back button.

- The Multifunction key serves several purposes, as described in this chapter. When the Settings (gear) icon is visible, as shown in Figure 4-1, tap the key to visit the Samsung Keyboard Settings screen.

- If you pine for a real keyboard, one that exists in the fourth dimension, you're not out of luck. See the nearby sidebar, "A real keyboard?"

- The keyboard reorients itself when you rotate the tablet. The onscreen keyboard's horizontal orientation is the easiest to use.

A real keyboard?

If typing is your thing but the onscreen keyboard doesn't do it for you, consider getting a real keyboard for your tablet. If Samsung doesn't offer a keyboard dock, get a Bluetooth keyboard. Even if the Bluetooth keyboard is labeled for that fruit company tablet, you can use it with your Galaxy Tab. Read more about Bluetooth in Chapter 16.

The Old Hunt-and-Peck

The purpose of the onscreen keyboard is to type, to generate text or input for the tablet. For the most part, using the keyboard makes sense. For the rest of the parts that don't make sense, turn to this section.

Typing one character at a time

Using the onscreen keyboard to type is simple: Tap a letter to produce the character. The keyboard makes a pleasant clicking sound as you type, and the tablet may vibrate slightly.

- To type in all caps, tap the Shift key twice. When the dot on the left Shift key is blue, Shift Lock is active. Tap the Shift key again to return to normal typing.

- Above all, it helps to type slowly until you get used to the onscreen keyboard.

- A blinking cursor on the touchscreen shows where new text appears, which is similar to how text input works on a computer.

- When you make a mistake, tap the Backspace key to back up and erase.

✔ On the Galaxy Tab S, tap the Del (delete) key to remove a character to the right of the cursor.

✔ When you type a password, each character you type appears briefly and is then replaced by a black dot for security reasons.

✔ See the later section, "Text Editing," for information on using the Ctrl (control) and arrow keys to edit text. These keys are unique to the Galaxy Tab S's keyboard.

Accessing special characters

You're not limited to typing only the symbols you see on the alphabetic keyboard (refer to Figure 4-1). The onscreen keyboard has many more symbols available, which you can see by touching the Sym key. Touching this key gives you access to two additional keyboard layouts, as shown in Figure 4-2.

Touch the 1/2 or 2/2 key to switch between the symbol keyboards, as illustrated in Figure 4-2. Some of the symbols may not look the same on all tablets.

To return to the standard alpha keyboard (refer to Figure 4-1), touch the ABC key.

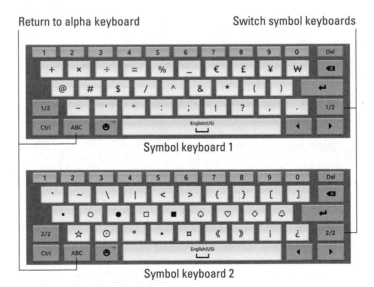

Figure 4-2: Number and symbol keyboards.

You can access special character keys from the main alphabetic keyboard, provided you know a secret: Long-press (touch and hold down) a key. When you do, you see a pop-up palette of additional characters, similar to the ones shown for the A key in Figure 4-3.

To access these characters, follow these steps:

1. **Long-press a key.**

   If a pop-up palette of alternative characters doesn't appear, the letter you pressed doesn't support this feature.

2. **Drag your finger up to the symbol you want to type.**

3. **Lift your finger to produce that character.**

If you make a mistake, you can't back out of the pop-up palette. In that case, just type the character, and then tap the Backspace key to erase it.

You can use this technique also to access the gray characters on the alphanumeric keyboard. For example, long-press the 7 key to access the & character.

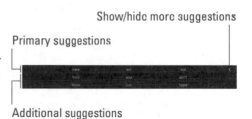

Figure 4-3: Special symbol pop-up palette thing.

Typing quickly by using predictive text

As you type, you may see a selection of word suggestions just above the keyboard. That's the tablet's Predictive Text feature. You can use this feature to greatly accelerate your typing.

In Figure 4-4, I typed the word *I*. The keyboard then suggested the words *have*, *am*, and *will*. Each of those is a logical choice for the next word after *I*. Additional choices are viewed by tapping the chevron, as called-out in the figure. Tap one of the suggested words to insert it in the text.

When your desired word doesn't appear, continue typing: The Predictive Text feature begins making suggestions based on what you've typed so far. Tap the desired word when it appears.

Show/hide more suggestions

Primary suggestions

Additional suggestions

Figure 4-4: Predictive Text in action.

To ensure that the Predictive Text has been activated on your tablet, follow these steps:

1. **Long-press the Multifunction key on the onscreen keyboard, and tap the Settings (gear) key.**

   The Multifunction key can change its function and appearance. If it already shows the Settings key (the gear icon shown in Figure 4-1), just tap that key.

2. **Ensure that the Master Control icon next to the Predictive Text option is on, or green.**

   Green means on. If the button isn't green, touch it to turn it green and activate Predictive Text.

3. **Press the Back button to return to your typing.**

Likewise, if you find Predictive Text boring and predictable, disable it by repeating these steps but turning off the Master Control in Step 2.

Adding keyboard swipe

If you're really after typing speed, consider enabling the onscreen keyboard's swipe feature. It allows you to type words by swiping your finger over the keyboard, like mad scribbling but with a positive result. To enable this feature, follow these steps when the onscreen keyboard is visible:

1. **Long-press the Multifunction key (labeled in Figure 4-1).**

2. **Choose the gear icon from the pop-up menu.**

3. **Choose Keyboard Swipe and ensure that Continuous Input is selected.**

   This step may involve two different taps, or you may just need to tap the Continuous Input item under the Keyboard Swipe heading.

When the keyboard swipe feature is active, you type by dragging your fingers over letters on the keyboard. Figure 4-5 illustrates how the word *hello* would be typed in this manner.

The keyboard swipe feature is disabled for typing a password or when using specific apps on the tablet. If it doesn't work, type one letter at a time.

Start here   End here

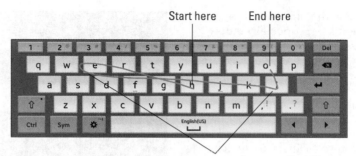

Keep your finger down as you drag over the letters

Figure 4-5: Using keyboard swipe to type *hello*.

Google Voice Typing

Your Galaxy tablet has the amazing capability to interpret your utterances as text. It works almost as well as computer dictation in science fiction movies, though I can't seem to find the command to destroy the planet Alderaan.

Activating voice input

To ensure that the tablet's dictation feature is active, obey these steps:

1. **Open the Settings app.**

2. **On the Galaxy Tab S, tap the General tab; on the Galaxy Tab 4, tap the Controls tab.**

   You would think that Samsung would show some consistency here.

3. **On the left side of the screen, choose Language and Input.**

4. **Ensure that a check mark is next to the option Google Voice Typing.**

   You're good.

Dictating text

Talking to your tablet really works, and works quite well, provided that you touch the Dictation key on the keyboard and properly dictate your text.

If you don't see the Dictation key, long-press the Multifunction key. (Refer to Figure 4-1 for the key's location.) Choose the microphone icon from the pop-up palette. The microphone icon replaces whatever icon was previously displayed.

To type with your voice, tap the Dictation key. A special window appears at the bottom of the screen, similar to what's shown in Figure 4-6. Dictate your text.

Accepting input

As you speak, the microphone icon flashes. The flashing doesn't mean that the tablet is embarrassed by what you're saying. No, the flashing merely indicates that your words are being digested.

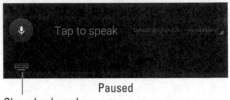

Paused

The text you utter appears as you speak. To pause, touch the Tap to Pause text on the screen. To use the keyboard, touch the keyboard icon (below the microphone icon, as shown in Figure 4-6). Or to continue dictation, touch the Tap to Speak text.

Show keyboard

Figure 4-6: Google Voice typing.

- ✐ The better your diction, the better your results.

- ✐ You can't use dictation to edit text. Text editing still takes place on the touchscreen, as described in the later section, "Text Editing."

- ✐ Speak the punctuation in your text. For example, you would say, "I'm sorry comma and it won't happen again" to produce the text *I'm sorry, and it won't happen again.*

- ✐ Common punctuation you can dictate includes the comma, period, exclamation point, question mark, colon, and new line (to start text on the next line).

- ✐ You can't dictate capital letters. If you're a stickler for such things, you'll have to go back and edit the text.

- ✐ Dictation may not work without an Internet connection.

*Uttering s**** words*

Your Galaxy Tab features a voice censor. Any naughty words you might utter are replaced; the first letter appears on the screen, followed by the appropriate number of asterisks.

For example, if *spatula* were a blue word and you uttered *spatula* when dictating text, the dictation feature would place *s******* on the screen rather than the word *spatula*.

Yeah, I know: silly. Or s****.

The tablet knows a lot of blue terms, including the infamous "Seven Words You Can Never Say on Television," but apparently the terms *crap* and *damn* are fine. Don't ask me how much time I spent researching this topic.

See Chapter 23 if you want the tablet to take naughty dictation.

Text Editing

You'll probably do more text editing on your Galaxy Tab than you realize. That editing includes the basic stuff, such as spiffing up typos and adding a period here or there as well as complex editing involving cut, copy, and paste. The concepts are the same as you find on a computer, but the process can be daunting without a keyboard and mouse. This section irons out the text-editing wrinkles.

Moving the cursor

The first part of editing text is to move the cursor to the right spot. The *cursor* is that blinking vertical line where text appears. On most computing devices, you move the cursor by using a pointing device. Your tablet has no pointing device, but you do: your finger.

To move the cursor, simply touch the spot on the text where you want the cursor to appear. To help your precision, a cursor tab appears below the text, as shown in the margin. Move that tab with your finger to move the cursor around in the text.

On the Galaxy Tab S, you can use the onscreen keyboard's left and right triangle keys to move the cursor. Tap the left triangle to move the cursor left one character; tap the right triangle to move right.

After you move the cursor, you can continue to type, use the Backspace key to back up and erase, tap the Del key to erase the character to the right, or paste text copied from elsewhere.

Selecting text

Selecting text on your Galaxy tablet works just like selecting text in a word processor: You mark the start and end of a block. That chunk of text appears highlighted on the screen. How you get there, however, can be a mystery — until now!

Start selecting by long-pressing the text or double-tapping a word. Upon success, you see a chunk of text selected, as shown in Figure 4-7.

Drag the start and end markers around the touchscreen to define the selected text.

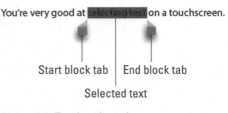

Figure 4-7: Text is selected.

To select all the text, touch the Select All command. It appears on the text selection action bar that appears whenever text is selected on your tablet. Two different action bars are used, Android and Samsung, as shown in Figure 4-8.

After you select the text, you can delete it by touching the Delete key on the keyboard. You can replace the text by typing something new. Or you can cut or copy the text. See the next section "Cutting, copying, and pasting."

- ✔ Selecting text on a web page works the same as selecting text in any other app. The big difference is that text can only be copied from the web page, not cut or deleted.

- ✔ On the Galaxy Tab S, you can select all text by tapping Ctrl+A on the onscreen keyboard: Press and hold down the Ctrl (control) key and tap the A key.

- ✔ To cancel the selection, touch the Done icon on the action bar, or just touch anywhere on the touchscreen outside the selected block.

Figure 4-8: Text selection action bar varieties.

Cutting, copying, and pasting

Selected text is primed for cutting or copying, which works just like it does in your favorite word processor. After you select the text, choose the proper command from the text selection action bar:

To copy the text, choose the Copy command.

To cut the text, choose Cut.

On the Galaxy Tab S, you can press Ctrl+C or Ctrl+X on the onscreen keyboard to copy or cut, respectively.

Just like on your computer, cut or copied text is stored in the Clipboard. To paste any previously cut or copied text, move the cursor to the spot where you want the text pasted.

If you're lucky, you'll see a Paste command button appear above the blinking cursor, as shown in Figure 4-9. Touch that command to paste the text.

Figure 4-9: The Paste command button.

If the Paste command button doesn't appear, touch the blue tab.

You can paste also by pressing Ctrl+V on the Galaxy Tab S's onscreen keyboard.

You can paste text only in locations where text is allowed. Odds are good that whenever you see the onscreen keyboard, you can paste text.

Viewing the clipboard

Another way to paste text is to use the Clipboard, shown in Figure 4-10.

Locked item   Hide the Clipboard   Remove items

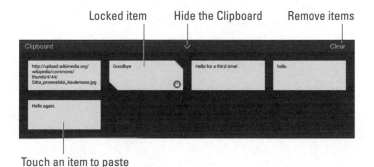

Touch an item to paste

Figure 4-10: The Clipboard.

To summon the Clipboard on the Galaxy Tab S, touch the clipboard icon on the onscreen keyboard's Multifunction key. The icon is shown in the margin. If you don't see that icon, long-press the Multifunction key and tap the clipboard icon.

On the Galaxy Tab 4, tap the Clipboard key to view the clipboard. That key is found in the lower-right corner of the keyboard.

The Clipboard lists items previously cut or copied, as shown in Figure 4-10. Tap an item to paste its contents into an app. You can continue to tap items and they'll be pasted as long as you like. When you're done, touch the down-pointing chevron to hide the Clipboard.

- Long-press an item to delete it or to lock it.

- To remove all items from the Clipboard, tap the Clear button. Tap the OK button to confirm.

- Locked items are not cleared when you clear the Clipboard. To remove a locked item, long-press it and choose the Unlock command. Then long-press again and choose the Delete command.

- A good item to lock into the Clipboard is your name and address. Once locked in the Clipboard, you can quickly paste that information into any app.

Undoing and redoing mistakes

If you've used a computer, you're most likely familiar with the Undo and Redo commands. The Galaxy Tab S offers the same commands, although only their keyboard shortcut versions are available: Ctrl+Z and Ctrl+Y.

- Tap the Ctrl+Z key combination to undo a previous action. This includes deleting text, moving text, and even typing new text.

- Tap the Ctrl+Y key combination to "undo the undo."

You can undo only the previous action. Unlike on a computer, you can't keep tapping Ctrl+Z to back up and erase multiple items.

Part II
Tablet Communications

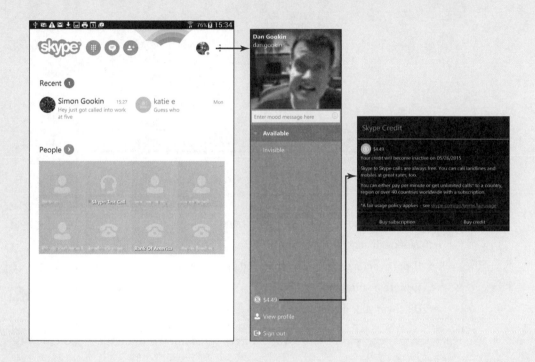

Recent ①

Simon Gookin   15:27
Hey just got called into work
at five

katie e   Mon
Guess who

People

In this part...

- Understand how to deal with your friends.
- Work with email on your Tab.
- Drool over text chat, video chat, and phone calls.
- Explore on the web.
- Discover your digital social life.

Bank Of America

All Your Friends in the Galaxy

In This Chapter

▶ Exploring the Contacts app

▶ Searching and sorting your contacts

▶ Adding new contacts

▶ Editing and changing contacts

▶ Updating a contact's picture

▶ Deleting contacts

*L*ong gone are the days when you had to keep a dozen or so phone numbers in your head. That was enough to call someone in a pinch. Beyond that, you kept an address book or scribbles on a kitchen cabinet. Now that everyone has a phone — and an email address, and a web page, and so on — keeping information about your friends all in your head is pretty much impossible. That's why your Galaxy Tab has an address book.

Meet the Tab's Address Book

The people you know, specifically those associated with your various online accounts, are accessed by using the Contacts app on your Galaxy Tab. It pulls in contacts from your Gmail account, plus other accounts you've added to the tablet. You can also manually add contacts. No matter how the people you know get there, the Contacts app is the place to look for them.

> ✔ If you haven't yet set up a Google account, refer to Chapter 2. That chapter also contains information on adding other accounts to your Tab.

> ✔ Many apps use contact information from the Contacts app, including Email, Gmail, Hangouts, as well as any app that lets you share information such as photographs or videos.

✔ Information from your social networking apps is also coordinated with the Contacts app. See Chapter 9 for more information on using the tablet as your social networking hub.

Using the Contacts app

To peruse your tablet's address book, open the Contacts app. It can be found on the Apps screen, or you may find a launcher icon for it on the Home screen.

Figure 5-1 illustrates important parts of the Contacts app. Tabs at the top left list contact categories; tap the Contacts tab to view everyone.

Use the index (on the left side of the screen, barely visible in Figure 5-1) to swiftly swipe through the list, or tap a letter to view contacts sorted by that letter. Tap a contact to view details, as shown on the right in Figure 5-1.

The list of activities you can do with a contact depends on the information shown and the apps installed on your Tab. Here are some common activities:

Place a phone call: The Galaxy Tab is not a phone, but if you install the Hangouts Dialer or a similar app, you can use the phone information to place a call. See Chapter 7 for details.

Send email: Touch the contact's email address to compose an email message using either the Gmail or Email app. When the contact has more than one

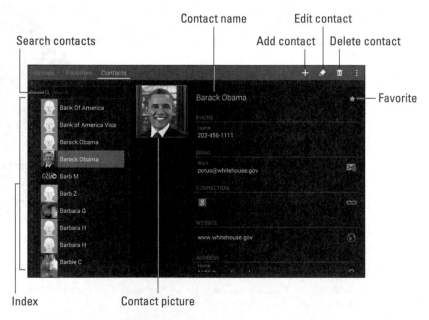

Figure 5-1: Your tablet's electronic address book.

email address, you can choose to which one you want to send the message. Chapter 6 covers email.

View address: When the contact lists a home or business address, you can tap that item to launch the Maps app to view the address. You can then get directions, look at the place using the Street View tool, or do any number of interesting things, covered in Chapter 10.

Some tidbits of information that show up for a contact don't have an associated action. For example, the tablet won't sing "Happy Birthday" when you touch a contact's birthday information.

- ✔ The Contact app on the Galaxy Tab 4 uses a white background, which is different from what's shown in Figure 5-1.

- ✔ Not every contact has a picture, and the picture can come from a number of sources (Gmail or Facebook, for example). See the section "Taking a picture of a contact."

- ✔ Also see the section "Joining identical contacts" for information on how to deal with duplicate entries for the same person.

Sorting your contacts

Perhaps you like the address book sorted by last name, but with the first name first. Or perhaps you want to see everyone last name first, but want them sorted by first name. Whatever the case, adjust the sort order by heeding these directions in the Contacts app:

1. **Tap the Action Overflow icon and choose Settings.**

2. **Choose Sort By.**

3. **Select First Name or Last Name, depending on how you want the list sorted.**

4. **Choose Display Contacts By.**

5. **Select First Name First or Last Name First to direct the app to display the names in the given manner.**

The Contacts app normally displays your address book first name first, sorted by first name.

Searching contacts

It's easy to find a contact by swiping the screen. It's easier to use the index to jump to a specific letter. When you have zillions of contacts, the best approach is to use the Search text box, shown in Figure 5-1.

Tap the Search text box. Use the onscreen keyboard to start typing a name. As you type, the list of contacts narrows until the exact person you're looking for is found.

Tap the X (cancel) button in the Search text box to clear the search.

No, there's no correlation between the number of contacts you have and how popular you are in real life.

Add More Friends

Having friends is great. Having more friends is better. Keeping all those friends as entries in Contacts is best.

Creating a contact from scratch

Sometimes it's necessary to create a contact when you actually meet another human being in the real world, or maybe you finally got around to transferring information to the Tab from your old paper address book. In either instance, you have information to input, and it starts like this:

1. **Touch the Add Contact icon in the Contacts app.**

   Refer to Figure 5-1 for the icon's specific location.

2. **Choose your Google account.**

   I recommend creating contacts associated with your Google account. That way the contacts are synchronized with the Internet and any other Android gizmos you may own. Or if you use another account as your primary account, such as Yahoo! choose it instead.

   Do not choose the Device item. When you do, the contact information is saved only on your Galaxy Tab. It won't be synchronized with the Internet or any other Android devices.

3. **Fill in information on the Create Contact form as best you can.**

   Fill in the text fields with the information you know: name, phone number and type (mobile, work, and so on), email address, and whatever other information you have.

4. **Tap the Add Another Field button to add additional fields, including Website.**

5. **Tap the Save button to add the contact.**

Providing that you followed my advice in Step 2, the new contact is automatically synced with your Google account. That's one beauty of the Android operating system used by the Galaxy Tab: You have no need to duplicate your efforts; contacts you create on the tablet are instantly updated with your Google account on the Internet.

Creating a contact from an email message

Perhaps one of the easiest ways to build up the Tab's address book is to create a contact from an email message. Follow these steps when you receive a message from someone not already in the address book:

1. **Tap the icon by the contact's name.**

   The Gmail app uses a letter icon for unknown contacts, such as the H shown in Figure 5-2. The Email app uses a generic human icon, also shown in the figure.

   Upon successfully tapping the icon, you'll see the card shown in Figure 5-2 on the right.

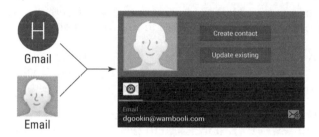

Figure 5-2: Adding a new email contact.

2. **Tap the Create Contact button.**

3. **Fill in the blanks on the Create Contact form.**

   The name and email address are already supplied for you — a bonus! Even if you don't know the rest of the info, you're still creating a contact. You can always add more details later; see the section, "Editing contact information."

4. **Ensure that your Google account is chosen for saving the contact.**

   If not, tap the action bar and choose Google Contact. Do not choose Device. Refer to the preceding section for my reason why Google is a good choice and Device is a poor choice.

5. **Tap the Save button to add the contact.**

When the email is from someone already in the address book, tap the Update Existing button in Step 2 (also refer to Figure 5-2). Scroll through the Contacts list to select the person, or the tablet may find the matching contact automatically. The new email address is added to that person's entry in the address book.

Importing contacts from your computer

Your computer's email program is doubtless a useful repository of contacts you've built up over the years. You can export these contacts from your computer's email program and then import them to the tablet. It's not easy, but it's possible.

The key is to save or export your computer email program's records in the *vCard* (.vcf) file format. These records can then be imported into the Contacts app. The method for exporting contacts varies depending on the email program:

In the Windows Live Mail program, choose Go ⇨ Contacts and then choose File ⇨ Export ⇨ Business Card (.VCF) to export the contacts.

In Windows Mail, choose File ⇨ Export ⇨ Windows Contacts and then choose vCards (Folder of .VCF Files) from the Export Windows Contacts dialog box. Click the Export button.

On the Mac, open the Address Book program and choose All Contacts. Then choose File ⇨ Export ⇨ Export vCard to save the vCards as a single file.

After the vCard files are created on your computer, transfer them from the computer to your Galaxy Tab. Directions for this process are covered in Chapter 17.

After the vCard files have been copied to the Tab, follow these steps in the Contacts app to complete the process:

1. **Tap the Action Overflow icon and choose Settings.**

2. **Choose Import/Export.**

3. **Choose Import from USB Storage.**

   If you've copied the contacts to the microSD card, choose Import from SD Card instead.

4. **Choose your Google account.**

5. **Select the Import All vCard Files option.**

6. **Touch the OK button.**

The contacts are not only saved in the tablet but also synchronized to your Google account, which instantly creates a backup copy.

The importing process may create some duplicates. That's okay: You can join two entries for the same person in the Contacts app. See the "Joining identical contacts" section, later in this chapter.

Grabbing contacts from your social networking sites

You can pour your whole gang of friends and followers from your social networking sites into the tablet. The operation is automatic: Simply add the social networking site's app to the tablet's inventory of apps as described in Chapter 9. At that time, you'll be prompted to sync the contacts or the apps will be added instantly to the Contacts app's address book.

Manage Your Friends

Nothing is truly perfect the first time, especially when you create things on a Galaxy Tab while typing with your thumbs at 34,000 feet during turbulence. You can do a whole slate of things with (and to) your friends in the tablet's address book. This section covers the more interesting and useful things.

Editing contact information

 To make minor touch-ups to any contact, locate and display the contact's information in the Contacts app. Tap the Edit icon (similar to the pencil icon shown in the margin), and start making changes.

Change or add information by touching a field and typing with the onscreen keyboard. You can edit information as well: Touch the field to edit and change whatever you want.

Some information cannot be edited. For example, fields pulled in from a social networking site can be edited only by the account holder on that social networking site.

When you've finished editing, tap the Save button.

Taking a picture of a contact

Nothing can be more delicious than snapping an inappropriate picture of someone you know and using the picture as his contact picture on your

Tab. Then every time he contacts you, that embarrassing, potentially career-ending photo comes up.

I suppose you could use nice pictures as well, but what's the fun in that?

To use the tablet's camera to snap a contact picture, heed these directions:

1. **Locate and display the contact's information.**

2. **Touch the contact's picture.**

   This trick works even when the picture is one of the boring generic images.

3. **Choose the Take Picture command.**

4. **Use the tablet's camera to snap a picture.**

   Chapter 11 covers using the camera. Both the front and rear cameras can be used (but not both at the same time). Tap the Shutter icon to take the picture.

5. **Review the picture.**

   Nothing is set yet. If you want to try again, tap the Retry button.

6. **Touch the OK or Save button to confirm the new image and prepare for cropping.**

7. **If you see a Complete Action Using, tap Crop Picture and then touch the Always button. Tap OK to confirm.**

   See Chapter 18 for more information on the Complete Action Using prompt.

8. **Crop the image, as shown in Figure 5-3.**

   Adjust the cropping box so that it surrounds only the portion of the image you want to keep.

9. **Touch the Done button to crop and save the image.**

   The image now appears whenever the contact is referenced on your tablet.

To remove an image from a contact, you need to edit the contact as described in the preceding section. Touch the contact's picture while you're editing, and then choose the Remove command.

You can also use any image stored on the tablet as a contact's picture. In Step 3, choose the Image command to view the Gallery. Browse for and select an image, and then crop.

Portion discarded   Portion kept   Save the cropped image

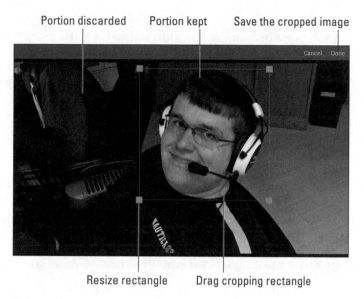

Resize rectangle   Drag cropping rectangle

Figure 5-3: Cropping a contact's image.

✔ For more information on the Complete Action Using prompt, see Chapter 18.

✔ See Chapter 12 for more information on the Gallery app.

Making a favorite

A *favorite* is a special type of contact, perhaps people you frequently stay in touch with, although not necessarily people you like. Making a contact a favorite places the person in the Favorites group, which is accessed by tapping the Favorites tab in the Contacts app (refer to Figure 5-1).

What about contact groups?

One of the tabs in the Contacts app is titled Groups. There you'll find any Google contact groups you've created. The problem is that you can't do anything with the groups. You would think that having a group would make it easier, for example, to send everyone an email message. Alas, contact groups don't work that way. They should, but they don't.

My advice is to ignore the contact groups.

To add a contact to the Favorites group, display the contact's information and touch the Favorite (star) icon by the contact's image. When the star is gold, the contact is one of your favorites and listed in the Favorites group.

To remove a favorite, touch the contact's star again, and it loses its color. Removing a favorite doesn't delete the contact.

By the way, a contact has no idea whether he's one of your favorites, so don't believe that you're hurting his feelings by not making him a favorite.

Joining identical contacts

The Galaxy Tab can pull in contacts from multiple sources (Facebook, Gmail, Twitter), so you may find duplicate contact entries. Rather than fuss over which to use, you can join similar contacts. Here's how:

1. **Wildly scroll the Contacts list until you locate a duplicate.**

   Well, maybe not *wildly* scroll, but locate a duplicated entry. Because the address book is sorted, duplicates usually appear close together.

2. **Select one of the duplicate contacts.**

3. **Tap the Action Overflow icon and choose Link Contact.**

   The card that appears lists some contacts that the tablet guesses could be identical. It might be spot-on. Also displayed is the entire Contacts list in case the tablet guesses incorrectly. Your job is to find the duplicate contact.

4. **Select the duplicate contact from the list.**

The accounts are merged, appearing as a single entry in the Contacts app.

Separating contacts

The topic of separating contacts has little to do with parenting, though separating bickering children is the first step to avoid a fight. Contacts in the address book might not be bickering, but occasionally the tablet may automatically join two contacts who aren't really the same person. When that happens, you can split them by following these steps:

1. **Display the contact that comes from two separate sources.**

   Sometimes it's difficult to spot such a contact. An easy way for me is when I see two diverse email addresses for the contact or an incorrect photo. Either situation could indicate a mismatch.

2. **Touch the Action Overflow icon and choose Separate Contact.**

    You see a list of contact sources, each with a red minus icon to the right.

    If you don't see the Separate Contact action, the contact you selected isn't joined, improperly or otherwise.

3. **Touch the red minus icon by the account you want to separate.**

4. **Tap the OK button to confirm.**

5. **Press the Back button when you're done.**

You don't need to actively look for improperly joined contacts as much as you'll just stumble across them. When you do, feel free to separate them, especially if you detect any bickering.

Removing a contact

Every so often, consider reviewing your contacts. Purge those folks whom you no longer recognize or have forgotten. It's simple: View the forlorn contacts and touch the Delete icon (similar to what's shown in the margin and also labeled in Figure 5-1). Tap the OK button to confirm. Poof! They're gone.

✔ Because the Contacts list is synchronized with your Google account, the contact is also removed there — and on other Android devices as well.

✔ For some linked accounts, the Contacts app won't let you delete the account. Instead, you need to remove the account from the linked source, such as Facebook.

✔ Removing a contact doesn't kill the person in real life.

Mail of the Electronic Kind

In This Chapter

▶ Configuring email on your tablet

▶ Receiving email

▶ Reading, replying to, and forwarding email

▶ Composing a new message

▶ Dealing with email attachments

▶ Changing your email signature

*T*ell someone that you don't have an email address and he'll look at you as if you just told him that you use candles at night instead of electric lights. Truly, having an email address is a sure sign that you're an active participant in the twenty-first century.

To help you meet your email and connectivity demands, the Galaxy Tab S provides two apps, Email and Gmail. This chapter uncovers their secrets and helps you get up and running with all your email accounts.

Google is updating the Gmail app so that it handles all your email. This update hasn't taken place as this book goes to press. If you notice any differences between this book's text and what you see on your tablet, visit my website for updates: www.wambooli.com/help/android/.

Galactic Email

Electronic mail is handled by two apps on your tablet: Gmail and Email.

The Gmail app hooks directly into your Google Gmail account. The app holds a copy of all the Gmail you send, receive, and archive. You access that mail just as you do on the Internet, by using the Gmail app on your tablet instead of a web browser.

The Email app connects with non-Gmail electronic mail, such as the standard mail service provided by your ISP, a web-based email system such as Yahoo! Mail or Windows Live Mail, as well as corporate email.

Regardless of the app, you work with electronic mail on your tablet just like you do on a computer: You can receive mail, create messages, forward email, send messages to a group of contacts, and work with attachments, for example. As long as an Internet connection is available, email works just peachy.

Adding the first email account

The Email app is used to access all your email from any account other than Gmail. The account types include web-based email, such as Yahoo! and Windows Live, as well as traditional ISP email, as you would get from Comcast, Cox, or any other major telecommunications corporation whose name begins with the letter *C*.

Getting things set up works the same no matter what type of account you have, although adding the first email account works differently. Obey these steps:

1. **Sacrifice a small animal to the moon goddess.**

   This step is optional and, in fact, is necessary only for those who are foolish enough not to buy this book.

2. **Open the Email app.**

   Look for it on the Apps screen, along with all the other apps on your tablet.

   The first screen you see is Set Up Email. If you've already run the Email app, you're taken to the Email inbox and you can skip these steps.

3. **Type your email address.**

   For example, if you have a Comcast email account, use the onscreen keyboard to type your *whoever@comcast.net* email address in the Email Address box.

   You'll find a .com key on the onscreen keyboard, which you can use to more efficiently type your email address. Look for it in the lower-right corner of the screen. And if you need .net or .org, long-press that key and choose the appropriate domain from the pop-up palette.

4. **Tap the Next button on the onscreen keyboard.**

5. **Type your email account's password.**

6. **Tap the Done key on the onscreen keyboard.**

   If you're lucky, everything connects smoothly, and you see the Account Options screen. Move on to Step 7.

If you're unlucky, you must specify some details on the Add Email Account screen. First double-check that you typed the proper email address and password. Also see the section, "Adding an account manually."

7. **Review the items on the Account Options screen.**

   You can change the schedule if you prefer to collect your email more frequently, although 15 minutes is pretty frequent.

8. **Tap the Next button, in the upper-right corner of the screen.**

   The button may appear as a right-pointing chevron.

9. **Give the account a name.**

   The account is given your email address as a name. If you want to change the name, type something new in that field. For example, I name my ISP's email account _Main_ because it's my main account.

10. **Confirm your own name.**

    The Your Name field shows your name as it's applied to outgoing messages. So if your name is really, say, Wilma Flagstone and not wflag4457, you can make that change now.

11. **Tap the Done button.**

    You're done.

After configuring the account, it's immediately synchronized with the tablet. You see the inbox and any unread, pending, or waiting messages. See the section "You've Got Email" for what to do next.

 If you use Yahoo! Mail, I recommend getting the Yahoo! Mail app for your Galactic tablet. That app handles your Yahoo! mail far better than the Email app, plus it gives you access to other Yahoo! features you may use and enjoy. The Yahoo! Mail app may be obtained from the Google Play Store. See Chapter 15.

Adding more email accounts

After you set up the first email account, different steps are required to add more email accounts. Here's how to add additional email accounts in the Email app:

1. **Tap the Action Overflow icon and choose Settings.**

2. **Tap Add Account.**

   This action is found on the left side of the screen, under the heading Account Settings.

3. **Proceed with the account setup and configuration.**

   Follow the steps in the preceding section, starting with Step 3.

The only change between adding a second email account and creating the first account is that you will be asked (after Step 5 in the preceding section) whether or not the new account is the primary or default account.

The new email account is synchronized immediately after it's added, and you'll see the inbox. Also see the later section, "Checking the inbox."

Adding an account manually

When the Email app doesn't recognize the email server, you'll have to manually add the account. You need to know the type of server: POP3, IMAP, or Microsoft Exchange. You'll also need to know other details, such as the server name, port address, domain name, and other highly technical information.

My advice is to contact your ISP or email provider: Look on their website for specific directions for connecting an Android tablet to the email account. Contact them directly if you cannot locate specific information.

The good news is that manual setup is rare these days. Most ISPs and web-mail accounts are added painlessly, as described earlier in this chapter.

Adding a corporate email account

I'm not being lazy, but the easiest way to set up your evil corporation's email on your tablet is to have the IT people do it for you. Or you may be fortunate and find directions on the organization's intranet. I present this tip because configuring corporate email, also known as Exchange Server email, can be a difficult and terrifying ordeal.

If you want to add the account on your own, first apply a secure screen lock, a PIN or Password lock, to the device. See Chapter 20 for details. You cannot have a corporate account without that higher level of security on the tablet.

Second, add the account as described in detail earlier in this chapter. Here are the general steps:

1. **Type your email address and password.**
2. **When prompted for the account type, choose Microsoft Exchange ActiveSync.**
3. **On the Exchange Server Settings screen, fill in the information.**

   This is the step where you need information from your evil organization's IT department. You need to know the domain, server name, and perhaps additional details too intimidating to specify here.
4. **Tap the OK button after ignoring the Activation warning message.**

5. **Tap the OK button if you see the Remote Security Administration warning.**

   The items on the Account Options screen are generally okay so:

6. **Tap the Next button.**

7. **Tap the Activate button if prompted to agree to the Device Administrator rules.**

   At this point, if you haven't yet applied a secure screen lock, you'll be prompted to do so.

8. **Name the account.**

   Feel free to change the account name to something more descriptive than your email address.

9. **Touch the Done button.**

Exchange Server accounts also synchronize your contacts, appointments, and other items from the organization. This synchronization affects the Contacts and Calendar apps on your Galaxy Tab S. Refer to Chapter 5 for information on the Contacts app; the Calendar app is covered in Chapter 14.

You've Got Email

New email arrives into your tablet automatically, picked up according to the Gmail and Email apps' synchronization schedules. Use the Gmail app to read your Google mail; use the Email app to read all other email. Yes, this is an annoying inconvenience. It will be fixed with the next release of the Gmail app, if Samsung chooses to install that release.

Receiving a new message

You're alerted to the arrival of a new email message in your tablet by a notification icon. The icon differs depending on the email's source.

 For a new Gmail message, the New Gmail notification (shown in the margin) appears at the top of the touchscreen.

 For a new email message, you see the New Email notification.

Pull down the notifications shade to review pending email. You see either a single notification representing the most recent message or a running total of the number of pending messages. Touch the notification to visit either the Gmail app or the Email app to read the message.

The Email app icon changes when new mail arrives. A value in an orange circle appears over the icon, which indicates the number of unread messages.

Checking the inbox

To peruse your Gmail, start the Gmail app. A typical Gmail inbox is shown in Figure 6-1.

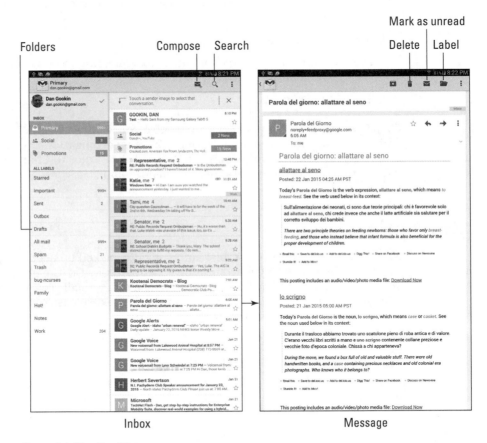

Figure 6-1: The Gmail inbox.

To check your Email inbox, open the Email app.

When you've configured the Email app for multiple email accounts, you can choose one from the action bar, shown in Figure 6-2. Or you can choose Combined View, which is what's shown in the figure.

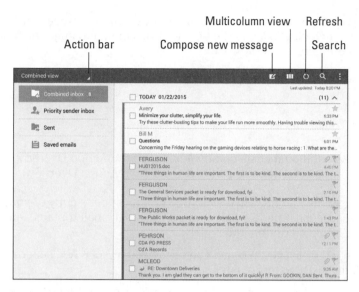

Figure 6-2: Messages in the Email app.

✔ Don't bother looking for your Gmail inbox in the Combined View window (refer to Figure 6-2). Gmail is its own app; your Gmail messages don't show up in the universal inbox.

✔ Multiple email accounts gathered in the Email app are color-coded. When you view the combined inbox, you see the color codes to the left of each message.

Reading email

As mail comes in, you can read it by choosing the new email notification, as described earlier in this chapter. Reading and working with the message operate much the same whether you're using the Gmail or Email app.

Touch a message to read it. The message text appears on the right side of the window or full screen, depending on how the tablet is oriented. Scroll the message up or down by using your finger.

To work with the message, use the icons that appear above the message. These icons, which may not look exactly like those shown in the margin, cover common email actions:

Reply: Touch this icon to reply to a message. A new message card appears with the To and Subject fields filled in based on the original message.

Reply All: Touch this icon to respond to everyone who received the original message, including folks on the Cc line. This command might be found by tapping the Action Overflow icon.

Forward: Touch this icon to send a copy of the message to someone else.

Delete: Touch this icon to delete the message.

To access additional email commands, touch the Action Overflow icon. For example, to print a message, choose Print from Action Overflow.

- ✔ Use Reply All only when everyone else must get a copy of your reply. Because most people find endless Reply All email threads annoying, use the Reply All option judiciously.

- ✔ Starred messages in Gmail can be viewed or searched separately, making them easier to locate later.

- ✔ If you properly configure the Email program, there's no need to delete messages you read. See the section "Configuring the server delete option," later in this chapter.

Write That Message

To get mail, you need to send mail. Send your Gmail messages by using the Gmail app. Send email from your other email accounts by using the Email app. Beyond that puzzling tidbit, the process works pretty much the same in both apps.

Composing a Gmail message

To create a new Gmail message, touch the Compose icon, shown in the margin. The Gmail composition screen appears, shown in Figure 6-3.

Touch the To field to enter the recipient's address; just type the first few letters and then choose a matching contact name.

Fill in the Subject field. Type the message. Touch the Send icon (labeled in Figure 6-3) to whisk off the message. Or if you'd rather save the message and work on it later, touch the Action Overflow icon and choose Save Draft.

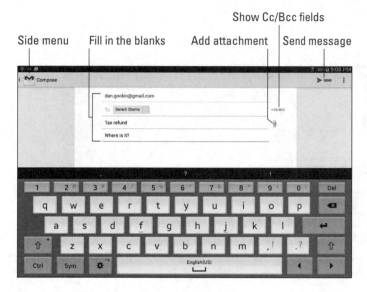

Figure 6-3: Writing a new Gmail message.

📌 To cancel a Gmail message, touch Action Overflow and choose Discard. Touch the Discard button to confirm.

📌 To work on a draft you've saved, touch the Side Menu icon (refer to Figure 6-3) and choose Drafts. Touch the draft message in the list, and then touch the Edit (pencil) icon to continue editing.

📌 To summon the Cc and Bcc fields, touch the +CC/BCC icon, as shown in Figure 6-3.

Crafting an Email message

To create a message in the Email map, touch the Compose icon (shown in the margin). The new message composition screen appears, similar to what you see in Figure 6-4.

Fill in the To field by typing a contact's name or email address. You need only type the first few letters of the name and then choose the person from the list — provided that the person's account is in the tablet's address book.

Type a subject, and then type the message's contents.

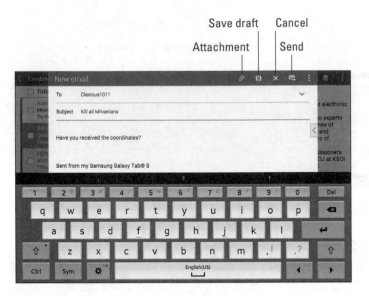

Figure 6-4: Composing al message in the Email app.

To send the message, touch the Send icon at the top of the composition window. Or you can touch the Save icon to save the message in the Drafts folder to edit and send later.

- ✔ Email is sent from your primary or default email account. See the later section, "Setting the primary email account."

- ✔ To cancel a message, touch the Cancel icon (refer to Figure 6-4). Touch Discard to confirm.

- ✔ Saved email is found in the Drafts folder associated with the email account you're using. Choose a specific inbox to view, and then select the Drafts folder from the left side of the screen. Then from the right side of the screen, choose the draft message to edit or send.

- ✔ You cannot see the Drafts folder unless you choose a specific account's inbox.

Sending email to a contact

A quick and easy way to compose a new message is to use the Contacts app to find a contact and then create a message using the contact's information. Heed these steps:

1. **Open the Contacts app.**

2. **Locate the contact to whom you want to send an electronic missive.**

3. **Touch the contact's email address.**

4. **Compose the message.**

At this point, creating the message works as described in the preceding sections.

You may be prompted with a Complete Action Using question after Step 3. If so, you'll see both the Gmail and Email apps listed. Choose one, then tap the Always button to always use that app. Also see Chapter 21 for information on what this prompt is for and how to potentially undo your selection, should you change your mind in the future.

Message Attachments

The key to understanding attachments in the Galactic email apps is to look for the paperclip icon, similar to what's shown in the margin. After you locate that icon, you can either deal with an attachment for incoming email or add an attachment to outgoing email.

Dealing with attachments

Attachments work differently between Gmail and Email. Either way, your goal is to either view or save the attachment. Sometimes you can do both!

Figure 6-5 shows both the Gmail app and Email app methods of dealing with an attachment. In the Gmail app, you can touch the paperclip icon to view the attachment, or touch the Action Overflow icon to choose whether to preview or save the attachment.

In the Email app, touch the Attachment tab in the message, shown in Figure 6-5. You can then touch the Preview button or the Save button to view the attachment or save it to the tablet's storage, respectively. When multiple items are attached, touch the Save All button.

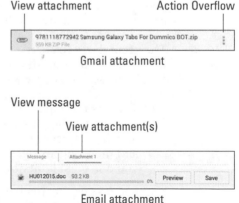

Figure 6-5: Attachment methods and madness.

The only snag you may encounter is one you may have on a computer as well: when nothing exists with which to open the attachment. When an app can't be found, you'll have to either suffer through not viewing the attachment or simply reply to the message and direct the person to resend the attachment in a common file format.

✔ Common file formats include PNG and JPEG for pictures, and HTML or RTF for documents. PDF, or Adobe Acrobat documents, are also common. Your Galaxy tablet should have no trouble opening them.

✔ Look for saved attachments by using the My Files app. Choose the Download History item from the left side of the screen to peruse recent downloads. Attachments you save may also generate a Download Complete notification icon; choose that notification to view the attachment.

Sending an attachment

You have two methods for sending an email attachment from your Galaxy Tab. The tablet way is to find the attachment and use a Share command to stick it in an email message. The traditional, computer way of sending an attachment is to first create the message and then attach the item.

Most apps that create or view information feature a Share command. Look for the Share icon, similar to what's shown in the margin. View the item you want to share — a picture, a video, music, a text message, or what-have-you — and then touch the Share icon. Choose the Gmail or Email app, and then compose your message as described in this chapter. The item you chose to share is automatically attached to the message.

The second way to share is to compose a new message and tap the paperclip icon, such as the one shown in Figure 6-4. Follow the directions on the screen to hunt down the attachment.

✔ When you compose a message and then add an attachment, you start by choosing the app that lets you access the attachment and then find the attachment itself. For example, to add a photo, choose the Gallery app and then look for the image you want to attach. Unlike using a computer, you don't just hunt down a specific file.

✔ It's possible to attach multiple items to a single email message. Just keep touching the attachment icon to add additional goodies.

✔ The variety of items you can attach depends on which apps are installed on the tablet.

✔ The Gmail and Email apps sometimes accept different types of attachments. So if you can't attach something by using the Gmail app, try using the Email app instead.

Email Configuration

You can have oodles of fun and waste oceans of time confirming and customizing the email experience on your Galaxy tablet. The most interesting things you can do are to modify or create an email signature, specify how mail you retrieve is deleted from the server, and assign a default email account for the Email app.

Creating a signature

I highly recommend that you create a custom email signature for sending messages from your tablet. Here's my signature:

```
DAN
This was sent from my Galaxy Tab.
Typos, no matter how hilarious, are unintentional.
```

To create a signature for Gmail, obey these directions:

1. **Start the Gmail app.**

2. **Tap the Action Overflow icon and choose Settings.**

3. **On the left side of the screen, choose your Gmail account.**

4. **On the right side of the screen, choose Signature.**

5. **Use the onscreen keyboard to type a signature.**

   If the account already has a signature, you can delete or edit it.

6. **Touch OK.**

In the Email app, you must set a separate signature for each email account:

1. **Tap the Action Overflow icon and choose Settings.**

   You may have to swipe the menu upward to scroll through the list of actions and find Settings.

2. **On the left side of the screen, select an account.**

3. **Choose Signature.**

4. **Type an email signature.**

5. **Touch the Done button.**

Repeat Steps 2 through 5 for each of your Email accounts.

Configuring the server delete option

ISP email that you fetch on your tablet is typically left on the email server. That's because the Email app, unlike a computer's email program, doesn't delete messages after it picks them up. The advantage is that you can retrieve the same messages later by using a computer. The disadvantage is that you end up retrieving mail you've already read and possibly replied to.

You can control whether the Email app removes messages after they're picked up. Follow these steps:

1. **Open the Email app.**

2. **Tap the Action Overflow icon and choose Settings.**

   You may need to swipe down the list of actions to locate Settings.

3. **On the left side of the screen, select a specific account.**

4. **Tap the More Settings button, at the bottom of the right side of the screen.**

5. **Choose Incoming Settings.**

   If you can't find the Incoming Settings item, you're dealing with a web-based email account, in which case there's no need to worry about the server delete option.

6. **Below the Delete Email from Server item, select the When I Delete from Inbox option.**

   The other option is Never. When chosen, the Never option keeps email on the server.

7. **Touch the Done button.**

Repeat Steps 3 through 7 for any additional email accounts you have.

After configuring the Delete Email from Server option, any message you delete in the Email app is deleted also from the mail server. The message isn't picked up again, not by the tablet, another mobile device, or any computer that fetches email from that same account.

- Mail you retrieve using a computer's mail program is deleted from the mail server after it's picked up. That's normal behavior. Your tablet cannot pick up mail from the server if your computer has already deleted it.

- Deleting mail on the server isn't a problem for Gmail. No matter how you access your Gmail, from a mobile device or from a computer, the inbox lists the same messages.

Setting the primary email account

When you have more than one email account, the main account — the default — is the one used by the Email app to send messages. To change that primary mail account, follow these steps:

1. **Start the Email app.**

2. **From the action bar, choose Combined View.**

3. **Tap the Action Overflow icon and choose Settings.**

4. **On the left side of the screen, select the email account you want to mark as your favorite.**

5. **On the right side of the screen, select the Default Account item.**

The messages you compose and send using the Email app are sent from the account you specified in Step 4.

7

Text Chat, Video Chat, and Even Phone Calls

In This Chapter

▶ Setting up Google Hangouts

▶ Chatting with friends

▶ Doing a voice chat

▶ Creating a Hangouts video chat

▶ Calling phones with the Hangouts app

▶ Texting with Skype

▶ Using Skype to make phone calls

The LTE Galaxy Tab has a phone number. It's not a dial-up phone number; your cellular provider merely uses the number to bill you. So as far as phone calls are concerned, you're as out-of-luck as owners of the Wi-Fi-only tablets. That's no cause for despair, however, because your Galactic tablet is more than capable of placing — and receiving — phone calls. All you need are the proper apps, which also provide tools for text chat, video chat, and even text messaging.

Let's Hang Out

One of the ways that you can fool your Galaxy Tab into acting more like a phone is to use the Hangouts app. It does text chat, voice, and video chat. It can even place phone calls, when properly equipped. The only downside to the app is that you can communicate only with your friends who have Google accounts.

Using Hangouts

The Hangouts app can be found on the Apps screen. You might also look for it inside the Google folder on the Home screen. And if you still can't find it, you can obtain the app from the Google Play Store. It's free! See Chapter 15.

When you first start the Hangouts app, it may ask if you want to make phone calls. Of course you do! Install the Hangouts Dialer — Call Phones app. If you're not prompted, get that app from the Play Store.

Hangouts hooks into your Google account. Contacts are listed on the far left tab. Previous conversations are listed on the right or center tab, as shown in Figure 7-1. The Phone Calls tab on the right appears only when you have the Hangouts Dialer app installed.

The Hangouts app listens for incoming conversation requests; you can also start your own. You can even do other things on the tablet — you'll be alerted via notification of an impending Hangout request.

To sign out of the app, which means you won't receive any notifications, tap the Side Menu icon (labeled in Figure 7-1) and choose Settings. Choose the Sign Out item on the right side of the screen. Tap OK to confirm.

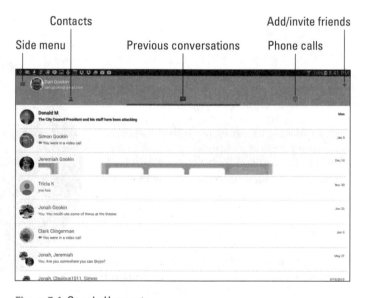

Figure 7-1: Google Hangouts.

✓ The Phone Calls tab, shown in Figure 7-1, appears only when the Hangouts Dialer is installed.

> ✓ Conversations are archived in the Hangouts app. To peruse a previous text chat, select it from the list. Video calls aren't archived, but you can review when the call took place and with whom.

> ✓ To remove a previous conversation, long-press it. Touch the Trash icon that appears atop the screen.

> ✓ Your friends can use Hangouts on a computer or a mobile device; it doesn't matter which. But they must have a camera available to enable video chat.

Typing at your friends

The most basic form of communication in the Hangouts app — and one of the oldest forms of communications on the Internet — is text chatting, in which people type text back and forth at each other. It can be most tedious. I'll be brief.

You start text chatting by following these steps in the Hangouts app:

1. **Tap the Contacts tab. Or to continue a previous conversation, tap the Previous Conversations tab.**

2. **Choose a contact or a previous conversation.**

3. **Use the onscreen keyboard to type a message, as shown in Figure 7-2.**

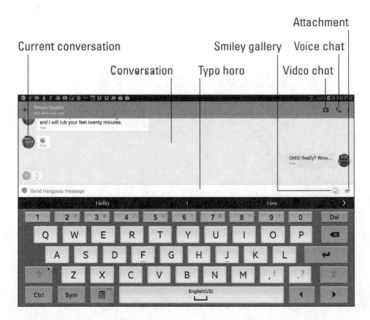

Figure 7-2: Text chatting.

4. **Touch the Send icon to send your comment.**

   The Send icon replaces the Attachment icon when you type a message.

You type, your friend types, and so on until you grow tired or the tablet's battery dies.

To chat with multiple friends, tap the Contacts tab and choose the first friend. Tap the Anyone Else button to add another contact. Keep choosing contacts until everyone you want is listed in the New Group Conversation window. When you're text chatting, or "hanging out," with a group, everyone in the group receives the message.

Adding more people to the hangout is always possible: During a chat, tap the Action Overflow icon and choose New Group Hangout. Tap a friend (only available friends are listed) to invite him in.

When someone sends you a text message by using the Hangouts app, you'll see a notification, similar to what's shown in the margin. Select that notification to review the message and begin a conversation.

Talking and video chat

Take the conversation up a notch by touching the Voice Chat icon on the text chat screen (labeled in Figure 7-2). Or — what the heck — tap the Video Chat icon and go for the full sensory overload. Either way, a notice shows up on the other person's screen, similar to the one shown in Figure 7-3. Tap the Answer button to begin talking.

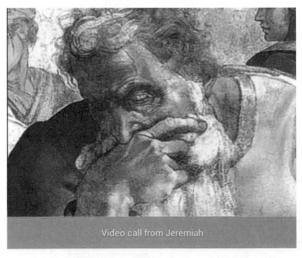

Video call from Jeremiah

Decline   Answer

Figure 7-3: Someone wants to video chat!

Figure 7-4 shows an ongoing video chat. The person you're talking with appears in the big window; you're in the smaller window. Other video chat participants, if they've been added, appear at the bottom-left of the screen, as shown in the figure.

Add contacts

Person you're calling   Switch cameras

Others in the hangout   Mute   Turn off video   You

Exit video chat

Figure 7-4: Video chat in the Hangouts app.

The onscreen controls (shown in Figure 7-4) may vanish after a second; tap the screen to see the controls again.

To end the conversation, touch the Exit Video Chat icon at the bottom center of the screen. Well, say "Goodbye" first, and then touch the button.

- When you're nude or just ugly, tap the Decline button for the video chat invite. Then choose that contact and reply with a text message or voice chat instead.

- When video chatting with multiple contacts, tap a contact from the bottom of the screen to see the person in a larger format in the center of the screen.

   The Tab's front-facing camera is at the top center of the tablet, the opposite end of the tablet as the Home button. If you want to make eye contact, look directly into the camera. When you do, however, you can't see the other video chat participants.

Placing a Hangouts phone call

If you've obtained the Hangouts Dialer app, you can use the Hangouts app to place a real live phone call. It's amazingly simple, and it works like this:

1. **Tap the Phone Calls tab in the Hangouts app.**

   Refer to Figure 7-1 for its location. If you don't see the Phone Calls tab, you haven't installed the Hangouts Dialer app yet.

2. **Type a contact name or a phone number.**

3. **Tap the matching contact, or tap the phone number (when it doesn't belong to a contact) to dial.**

   The call is placed.

Tap the red End Call icon when you're done.

- ✔ To the person you're calling, an incoming Hangouts call looks just like any other call, although the number may be displayed as *Unavailable*.

- ✔ The good news: Calls are free!

- ✔ The bad news: Not every number can be dialed by using the Hangouts app.

Connect to the World with Skype

More popular and ancient than the Hangouts app is Skype. It's the traditional way to place phone calls on the Internet, including inexpensive international calls. Despite the growing popularity of Google Hangouts, Skype remains one of the most popular Internet communications tools.

Getting Skype for your Tab

Your Galaxy Tab most likely didn't come with the Skype app, so visit the Google Play Store and obtain the app. If you find multiple Skype apps, get the one from the Skype company itself.

To use Skype, you need a Skype account. If you already have one, sign in when you first start the app. Otherwise, you can sign up when the app starts.

- ✔ When you start the Skype app for the first time, work through the start-up screens. You can even take the tour. Be sure to have Skype scour the tablet's address book (the Contacts app) for contacts who you can Skype. This process may take a while, but if you're just starting out, it's a great help.

✔ Skype is free to use. Text chat is free. Voice and video chat with one other Skype user is also free. But if you want to call a real phone or video chat with a group, you need to boost your account with Skype Credit.

✔ You can use video chat with Google Hangouts without having to pay extra.

✔ Don't worry about getting a Skype number, which costs extra. It's necessary only if you expect to receive phone calls on your tablet by using Skype.

Chatting with another Skype user

Text chat with Skype works similarly to texting on a smartphone. The only difference is that the other person must be a Skype user. So in that respect, Skype text chat works a lot like Google Hangouts chat, covered elsewhere in this chapter.

To chat, follow these steps:

1. **Start the Skype app and sign in.**

   You don't need to sign in when you've previously run the Skype app. Like all other apps, Skype continues to run until you sign out or turn off the tablet.

2. **At the main Skype screen, tap the People icon and choose a contact.**

   Or you can choose one of the recent contact icons shown on the main screen.

3. **Type your text in the text box.**

   The box is found at the bottom of the screen. It says *Type a Message Here.*

4. **Touch the blue arrow to send the message.**

   As long as your Skype friend is online and eager, you'll be chatting in no time.

You don't need to formally end your chat session. Switch away to another app or lock the tablet. A Skype notification, shown in the margin, floats in should the other party continue the conversation. You'll also see the Skype notification when someone else initiates a chat with you.

Seeing on Skype (video call)

Placing a video call with Skype on your Galaxy tablet is easy: Begin a text chat as described in the preceding section. After the conversation starts, tap the Video Call icon, as shown in the margin. The call rings through to the contact, and if the person wants to video chat, he picks up in no time and you're talking and looking at each other.

Placing a Skype phone call

Ah. The big enchilada: Skype can be used to turn your Galaxy Tab — be it LTE or Wi-Fi — into a smartphone. It's an amazing feat. And it works quite well, providing you have Skype Credit.

To ensure that you have Skype Credit, touch your Account icon on the main Skype screen, shown in Figure 7-5. Touch the Skype Credit item to see a summary of the credit and potentially get more, as illustrated in the figure.

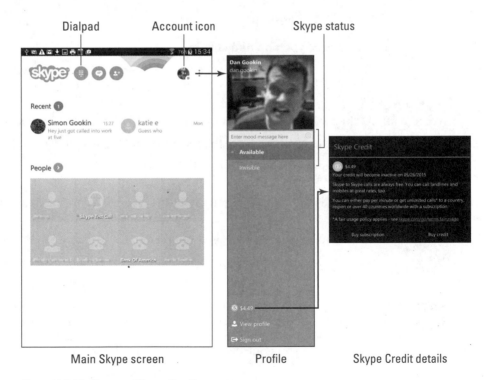

Main Skype screen   Profile   Skype Credit details

Figure 7-5: Finding your Skype Credit.

If you have Skype Credit, you can use the tablet to make a "real" phone call, which is a call to any phone number on the planet (planet earth). Heed these steps:

1. **Choose a contact to call.**

   Your Skype contact must have a phone number listed in his contact information. Otherwise, you'll have to dial the number directly, which is described near the end of this section.

2. **Touch the Phone icon, in the upper-right corner of the screen.**

   If you don't see the Phone icon, the contact's information doesn't include a real live phone number.

3. **Talk.**

   The Call screen looks similar to the one in Figure 7-6.

4. **To end the call, touch the red End Call button.**

   Refer to Figure 7-6 for the button's location.

To dial a number not associated with a contact, touch the Dialpad icon at the top of the main Skype screen (refer to Figure 7-5, left). Punch in the number to dial, starting with 1 (for the United States), then the area code, and then the number. Touch the green Dial icon to place the call.

Lamentably, you can't receive a phone call using Skype unless you pay for a Skype online number. In that case, you can use Skype to both send and receive regular phone calls. This book doesn't cover the Online Number option.

- ✔ I recommend getting a good headset if you plan to use Skype often to place phone calls.

- ✔ In addition to having to pay the per-minute cost, you may be charged a connection fee for making the call.

Mute   Dialpad   End call

Figure 7-6: Calling a real phone by using Skype.

✔ You can check the Skype website (www.skype.com) for a current list of call rates, for both domestic and international calls.

✔ Unless you've paid Skype to have a specific phone number, the phone number shown on the recipient's Caller ID screen is something unexpected — often, merely the text *Unknown.* You might therefore want to email the person you're calling and let her know that you're placing a Skype call. That way, the call won't be skipped because the Caller ID isn't recognized.

8

Web Browsing

In This Chapter

▶ Browsing the web
▶ Adding a bookmark
▶ Working with tabs
▶ Sharing web pages
▶ Downloading images and files
▶ Setting a new home page
▶ Configuring the web browser

The World Wide Web was designed to be viewed on a computer. The monitor is big and roomy. Web pages are displayed amply, like Uncle Ron on the sofa watching a ballgame. The smaller the screen, the more difficult it is to view web pages designed for those roomy monitors. The web on a smartphone? Tragic. But on a Galaxy Tab?

The Galaxy family of tablets comes in a variety of sizes. Even the smallest cousin sports a screen large enough to make viewing information on the web enjoyable. It's like seeing a younger, thinner version of Uncle Ron sitting on the Hepplewhite. The web on your tablet can be a pleasure to witness, especially when you've read the good information in this chapter.

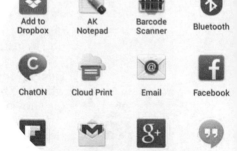

▶ If you have an LTE Tab, activate the Wi-Fi connection before you venture out on the web. Although you can use the mobile data connection, the Wi-Fi connection incurs no data usage charges.

▶ Many places you visit on the web can instead be accessed more effectively by using specific apps. To visit Facebook, Gmail, Twitter, YouTube, and other popular online services, use an app instead of visiting the website. Check the Google Play Store to see whether or not your favorite website has its own app.

The Web Browser App

The Galaxy Tab comes with two web browser apps: Internet and Chrome.

Internet is Samsung's web browser. It's essentially the Chrome app but all gussied up by Samsung. That's the web browser app covered in this chapter.

Chrome is Google's web browser app, the default web browser app for all Android devices. My guess is that future releases of the Galaxy Tab will feature Chrome exclusively.

If you use Chrome on a computer, use Chrome on your Tab. You'll find the same bookmarks and browser history shared between all devices that use the Chrome browser.

Mobile Web Browsing

Rare is the person these days who has had no experience with the World Wide Web. More common is someone who has used the web on a computer but has yet to taste the Internet waters on a mobile device. If that's you, consider this section your quick mobile web orientation.

Viewing the web

To browse the web on your Galaxy Tab, open the Internet app. It's found on the Apps screen, or you might be lucky and locate an Internet app launcher icon on the Home screen.

The first time you fire up the Internet app, you may see the Samsung registration page. Register your tablet to receive sundry Samsung bonus stuff — or not. Registration is optional.

Figure 8-1 illustrates the Internet app's interface. The same features appear when the tablet is oriented vertically, although when oriented horizontally (as shown in Figure 8-1), web pages look better.

Here are some handy tablet web-browsing tips:

✐ Pan the web page by dragging your finger across the touchscreen. You can pan up, down, left, or right when the page is larger than the tablet's screen.

✐ Pinch the screen to zoom out and spread two fingers to zoom in.

✐ The page you see may be the mobile page, or a customized version of the web page designed for small-screen devices. To see the non-mobile version, tap the Action Overflow icon and choose Desktop View.

✔ See the later section, "Setting a home page," for information on choosing a home page (also a new tab page) other than Samsung's page.

✔ I confess that the name *Internet* is rather silly for a web browser app. It's not the silliest. I've seen Android tablets with a web browser app named Web. Then again, Chrome doesn't make much sense, either.

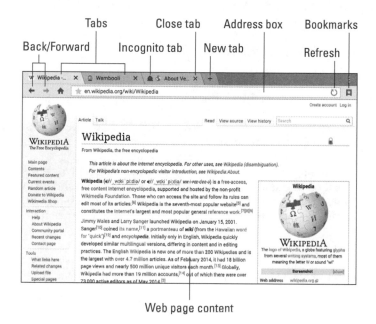

Figure 8-1: The Internet app.

Visiting a web page

To visit a web page, type its address into the Address box (labeled in Figure 8-1). You can also type a search word or phrase if you don't know an exact web page address. Tap the Go button on the onscreen keyboard to search the web or to visit a specific web page.

If you don't see the Address box, touch the web page's tab atop the screen. The Address box, along with the various buttons left and right, appears on the screen. If that doesn't work, swipe the screen from top-to-bottom.

You "click" links on a page by touching them with your finger. If you have trouble stabbing the right link, zoom in on the page and try again. Sometimes a tiny magnifier appears when tapping a link. It helps you poke the right item, although you can't control when and how the magnifier appears.

✔ When typing a web page address, use the onscreen keyboard's `www.` key to instantly type those characters for the address. The `www.` key changes to the .com key to assist you in rapidly typing those characters as well. Long-press that key to see other domains, such as .org and .net.

✔ To reload a web page, touch the Refresh icon on the right end of the Address box.

✔ To stop a web page from loading, touch the X that appears to the right of the Address box. The X replaces the Refresh icon.

Browsing back and forth

To return to a web page, you can tap the Internet app's Back icon (labeled in Figure 8-1) or press the tablet's Back button (shown in the margin).

Tap the Internet app's Forward icon to go forward or to return to a page you were visiting before you touched the Back icon.

To review the long-term history of your web-browsing adventures, tap the Bookmarks icon in the upper-right corner of the screen (shown in the margin and in Figure 8-1). Select the History tab to view your web-browsing history. Select a web page from the History list to view a page you visited weeks or months ago.

✔ See the later section, "Clearing your web history," for information on purging items from the History list.

✔ Also see the section, "Managing web pages in multiple tabs," for information on going incognito.

✔ By the way, if you're prompted to use your Samsung account to back up your bookmarks, just cancel. You don't need a Samsung account to use your Galaxy Tab.

Working with bookmarks

Bookmarks are those electronic breadcrumbs you can drop as you wander the web. Need to revisit a website? Just look up its bookmark. This advice assumes, of course, that you bothered to create a bookmark when you first visited the site. Bother with these steps in the Internet app:

1. **Navigate to the web page you must bookmark.**

2. **Tap the Bookmarks icon and ensure that the Bookmarks tab is selected.**

3. **Tap the Add button.**

   The Add Bookmark card appears, shown in Figure 8-2. All the fields are preset for you, although you may not be entirely pleased with the settings.

4. **If you're an organized person, tap the Folder button (refer to Figure 8-2) to set a specific folder for the bookmark.**

   You can organize your bookmarks later by viewing the bookmarks in the Internet app and then tapping the Edit key. This type of in-depth organization is optional.

5. **Type or edit the bookmark's name.**

   I prefer short, punchy names as opposed to long, meandering text.

6. **Tap the Save button to create the bookmark.**

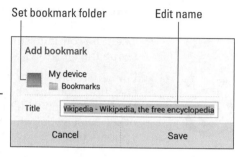

Figure 8-2: Creating a bookmark.

After the bookmark is set, it appears on the Bookmarks tab. To see all your bookmarks, tap the Bookmarks icon on the Internet app's main window (refer to Figure 8-1). Next, choose the Bookmarks tab. Tap a bookmark to visit that page.

✔ Remove a bookmark by long-pressing its entry in the Bookmarks list. Choose the Delete command or the Delete Bookmark command. Tap the OK button to confirm. The bookmark is gone.

✔ Bookmarked websites can also be placed on the Home screen: Long-press the bookmark thumbnail and choose Add Shortcut to Home.

Managing web pages in multiple tabs

The Internet app uses a tabbed interface to display more than one web page at a time. Refer to Figure 8-1 to see various tabs marching across the Internet app's screen, just above the Address box.

Here's how you work the tabbed interface:

✔ *To open a new tab,* touch the plus button to the right of the last tab. The tab opens using the home page set in the Internet app. See the later section, "Setting a home page."

✔ *To open a link in a new tab,* long-press that link. Choose the Open in New Tab action.

✔ *To open a bookmark in a new window,* long-press the bookmark and choose the Open in New Tab action.

You switch between tabs by choosing one from the top of the screen.

Close a tab by touching its X (Close) icon.

- The tabs continue sprouting across the screen, left to right. You can swipe the tabs to view the ones that have scrolled off the screen.

- For secure browsing, you can open an *incognito tab:* Tap the Action Overflow icon and choose New Incognito Tab. When you go incognito, the Internet app won't track your history, leave cookies, or provide other evidence of which web pages you've visited. A short description appears on the incognito tab page, describing how it works.

Searching in and on the web

The handiest way to find things on the web is to use the Google Now app, covered in Chapter 14. You can also find a Google Search widget on the Primary Home screen. If not, refer to Chapter 18 for information on adding the Google Search widget.

While you're using the Internet app, use the Address box to search; type search text and tap the Go button on the onscreen keyboard. Tap the action bar to the left of the Address box (the action bar replaces the Home icon) to choose a search engine.

To locate text on a web page, tap the Action Overflow icon and choose Find on Page. Type the search text in the Find on Page box. As you type, found text is displayed on the screen. Use the up and down triangle buttons to page through the document. Press the Back button to dismiss the toolbar after you've finished searching.

Sharing a page

There it is! That web page that you just *have* to talk about to everyone you know. The gauche way to share the page is to copy and paste it. Because you're reading this book, though, you know the better way to share a web page. Heed these steps:

1. **Go to the web page you desire to share.**

2. **Tap the Action Overflow icon and choose Share Via.**

   A list of sharing apps appears. The variety and number of apps depend on the apps installed on your tablet.

3. **Choose an app.**

   For example, choose Gmail to send the link by email, or choose Facebook to share the link with your friends.

4. **Do whatever you should do next.**

   Whatever you should do next depends on how you're sharing the link: Compose the email, write a comment in Facebook, or whatever. Refer to various chapters in this book for specific directions.

You cannot share a page you're viewing on an incognito tab.

The Art of Downloading

There's nothing to downloading, other than understanding that most people use the term incorrectly. Officially, a *download* is a transfer of information over a network from another source to your gizmo. For a Galaxy Tab, that network is the Internet, and the other source is a web page.

- ✔ The download notification appears after the tablet has downloaded something. Choose that notification to view the download.

- ✔ Nope, you never download programs to your tablet. That's because new apps are obtained from the Google Play Store. See Chapter 15.

- ✔ Most people use the term *download* to refer to copying or transferring a file or other information. That's technically inaccurate, but the description passes for social discussion.

- ✔ The opposite of downloading is *uploading.* That's the process of sending information from your gizmo to another location on a network.

Grabbing an image from a web page

Downloading an image from a web page is cinchy: Long-press the image. You see a pop-up menu, from which you choose the Save Image action.

To view images you download from the web, you use the Gallery app. Downloaded images are saved in the Download album. Refer to Chapter 12 for information on the Gallery app.

Downloading a file

Your Galaxy Tab tries its best to view some types of links, such as PDF files. When you'd rather save the linked information, long-press the link and choose the Save Link action. The linked file is downloaded to your tablet.

If the Save Link command doesn't appear, the file cannot be downloaded, either because the file is an unrecognized type or because there is a potential security issue.

Finding the downloads

The easiest way to locate downloaded material is to choose a download notification, similar to what's shown in the margin. The downloaded item opens by using whatever app opens it best, although sometimes you'll see the Complete Action Using prompt. In that case, choose an app to view the download.

To review the items you've downloaded in one location, use the My Files app. Open the app and choose the Download History item from the left side of the screen. You see a list of all items downloaded, including saved images, links, and files from the web.

✔ For more information on the Complete Action Using prompt, see Chapter 18.

✔ Downloads are stored in the Download folder on the tablet's internal storage device. You can browse to that folder in the My Files app by choosing Device Storage and then Download from the left side of the screen.

Internet App Controls and Settings

More options and settings and controls exist for the Internet app than just about any other app I've used on a Galaxy Tab. It's complex. Rather than bore you with every dangdoodle detail, I thought I'd present just a few of the options worthy of your attention.

Setting a home page

The *home page* is the first page you see when you start the Internet app, and it's the first page that's loaded when you fire up a new tab. To set a home page, heed these directions:

1. **Browse to the page you want to set as the home page.**

2. **Tap the Action Overflow icon and choose Settings.**

3. **On the left side of the screen, choose Set Home Page.**

4. **On the right side of the screen, choose Current Page.**

   Now you see why I had you browse to the page in Step 1.

The home page is set.

If you want your home page to be blank (not set to any particular web page), choose Other in Step 4. In the text box on the Set card, type **about:blank**. Tap the OK button.

I prefer a blank home page because it's the fastest web page to load. It's also the web page with the most accurate information.

Clearing your web history

When you don't want the entire Internet to know what you're looking at on the web, open an incognito tab, as described earlier in the section, "Managing web pages in multiple tabs." When you forget to do that, follow these steps to clear one or more web pages from the browser history:

1. **Tap the Bookmarks icon.**

2. **Tap the History tab.**

3. **Touch the Edit button.**

4. **Long-press a web page entry to select it.**

5. **Tap other items to select them as well.**

6. **Tap the Delete (trash can) icon atop the screen.**

    The evidence is erased.

Each time you do this, remind yourself, "Next time, I'll remember to use the incognito tab." Web pages you visit while incognito are not recorded in the browser's history.

Changing the way the web looks

No matter which size Galactic tablet you own, you have several ways to improve the way the web looks. First and foremost, don't forget that you can orient the device horizontally or vertically, which rearranges the way a web page is displayed.

From the Settings screen, you can also adjust the zoom setting used to display a web page. Heed these steps when using the Internet app:

1. **Tap the Action Overflow icon and choose Settings.**

2. **On the left side of the screen, choose Screen and Text.**

3. **On the right side of the screen, use the Text Scaling slider to adjust the text scaling.**

You can spread your fingers to zoom in on any web page.

Setting privacy and security options

As far as the Internet app's settings go, most of the security options are already enabled, including the blocking of pop-up windows (which normally spew ads).

If information retained on the tablet concerns you, you can clear it when you use the Internet app. Obey these steps:

1. **Tap the Action Overflow icon and choose Settings.**

2. **Choose Privacy from the left side of the screen.**

3. **Remove check marks by the items Remember Form Data and Remember Passwords.**

4. **Tap the Delete Personal Data item.**

5. **Place check marks by each item on the Delete Personal Data card.**

6. **Tap the Done button.**

With regard to general online security, my advice is always to be smart and think before doing anything questionable on the web. Use common sense. One of the most effective ways that the Bad Guys win is by using *human engineering* to try to trick you into doing something you normally wouldn't do, such as click a link to see a cute animation or a racy picture of a celebrity or a politician. As long as you use your noggin, you should be safe.

Also see Chapter 20 for information on applying a secure screen lock to your Tab.

The Digital Social Life

In This Chapter

▶ Accessing social updates for your contacts

▶ Getting Facebook

▶ Sharing your life on Facebook

▶ Sending pictures to Facebook

▶ Tweeting on Twitter

▶ Exploring other social networking opportunities

*T*he Internet is amazing. It has greatly expanded mankind's access to knowledge, while proving to be the largest time-killer in history. Marching forward in support of the second hypothesis, I present you with the topic of social networking.

Armed with your Galaxy tablet, you can keep your digital social life up-to-date wherever you go. You can communicate with your friends, followers, and buddies; upload pictures and videos you take on the tablet; or just share your personal, private, intimate thoughts with the mass of humanity.

Face to Face with Facebook

Of all the social networking sites, Facebook is the king. It's the online place to go to catch up with friends, send messages, express your thoughts, share pictures and videos, play games, and waste more time than you ever thought you had.

✔ Although you can access Facebook on the web by using the tablet's web browser app, I highly recommend that you use the Facebook app, described in this section.

✔ Future software updates to your Galaxy tablet may include a Facebook app or another social networking app. If so, you can read an update on my website at www.wambooli.com/help/galaxytabs/.

Getting the Facebook app

As this book goes to press, no Galaxy tablet comes with a Facebook app. Fret not! You can get the Facebook app free from the Google Play Store. That app is your red carpet to the Facebook social networking kingdom.

To get the Facebook app, obey these steps:

1. **Visit the Google Play Store, and search for and obtain the Facebook app.**

   If you need specific directions, see Chapter 15, which covers using the Play Store app.

2. **Open the Facebook app and log in by using your Facebook user name and password.**

   Or you can tap the item Sign Up for Facebook to set up a new account.

You may see a notification asking for the tablet to access your Facebook account. Feel free to ignore this request. Approving it allows the tablet to automatically update your Facebook status, which is probably not something you would want.

Synchronizing Facebook contacts

To ensure that your Facebook contacts are found in the tablet's Contacts app, follow these steps:

1. **Open the Settings app.**
2. **Tap the General tab.**
3. **Choose Accounts on the left side of the screen.**
4. **Tap Facebook on the right side of the screen.**
5. **Tap your email address on the right side of the screen.**

   The text Sync Turned Off should appear below that account. If not, you see a timestamp for the previous sync. Continue anyway with these steps.

6. **Place a check mark by the item Sync Contacts.**
7. **If you'd like to synchronize Facebook events with the tablet's Calendar app, place a check mark by the item Sync Calendar.**
8. **Tap the Home button when you've finished making settings.**

Facebook accounts appear in the Contacts app along with your Google and other contacts. See Chapter 5 for details.

See Chapter 14 for information on the Calendar app.

Running Facebook on your tablet

You access Facebook by running the Facebook app. If you can't find the Facebook app, you need to install it; refer to the preceding section.

Log into your Facebook account, if prompted. You stay logged into Facebook as long as the tablet is on or until you log out.

The main Facebook screen has several tabs, as shown in Figure 9-1. The primary tab is the News Feed. Options for interacting with Facebook appear at the bottom of the screen.

When you need a respite from Facebook, press the Home button to return to the Home screen.

To log out of the Facebook app, tap the More icon (refer to Figure 9-1) and choose the Log Out command (from the bottom of the list). Tap the Log Out button to confirm.

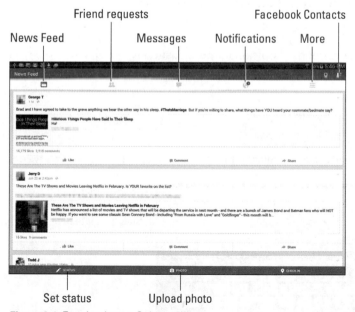

Figure 9-1: Facebook on a Galaxy tablet.

> ✔ Refer to Chapter 19 for information on placing a Facebook app or widget on the Home screen.
>
> ✔ Use the Like, Comment, or Share buttons below a News Feed item to comment, like, or share something, respectively. You can see any existing comments only when you choose the Comment item.
>
> ✔ Update the News Feed by swiping the screen downward.

Setting your status

The primary thing you live for on Facebook, besides having more friends than anyone else, is to update your status. It's the best way to share your thoughts with the universe, far cheaper than skywriting and far less offensive than a robocall.

To set your status, follow these steps in the Facebook app:

1. **Switch to the News Feed.**

   Tap the News Feed icon, labeled in Figure 9-1.

2. **Touch the Status button at the top of the screen.**

   You see the Write Post screen, where you can type your musing, similar to what's shown in Figure 9-2.

3. **Tap the To field to set the post's visibility.**

   The two main options are Public and Friends, where Public makes the post visible to anyone on Facebook and Friends limits viewing to only your friends. Additional options, such as groups and locations, are made available by tapping the More command.

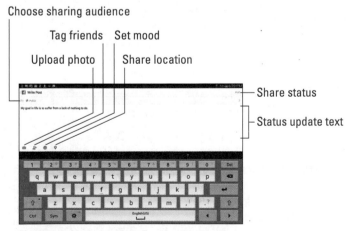

Figure 9-2: Updating your Facebook status.

4. **Tap the What's On Your Mind field to type something pithy, newsworthy, or typical of the stuff you read in Facebook.**

   When you can't think of anything to post, take off your shoes, sit down, and take a picture of your feet against something else in the background. That seems to be really popular.

5. **Tap the Post button to share your thoughts.**

You can also set your status by using the Facebook widget on the tablet's Home screen, if it's been installed. Touch the What's on Your Mind text box, type your important news tidbit, and then touch the Share button.

To cancel a post, tap the Back button. Tap the Discard button to confirm.

Uploading a picture to Facebook

One of the many things your Galaxy tablet can do is take pictures. Combine that feature with the Facebook app, and you have an all-in-one gizmo designed for sharing the various intimate and private moments of your life with the ogling throngs of the Internet.

The picture-posting process starts by touching a Photo icon in the Facebook app. Refer to Figures 9-1 for the Photos icon's location on the News Feed screen. After touching the Photo icon, you see the photo selection screen. You have two choices:

- ✔ First, you can select an image from those found on the tablet. Touch an image, or touch several images to select a bunch, and then proceed with the steps listed later in this section.

- ✔ Second, you can take a picture by using the tablet's camera; tap the Add Photo icon in the upper-right corner of the screen (and shown in the margin).

If you elect to use the tablet's camera to take a picture, you'll be switched to the Camera app. Snap the photo. Tap OK to accept the image, or tap the Retry button to try again. After tapping OK, the image is ready to post to Facebook, as shown in Figure 9-3.

Figure 9-3: Adding an image to Facebook.

After selecting the image, it appears on the Write Post screen. Continue to create the post as described earlier in this chapter. Then tap the Post button. The image can be found as part of your status update or News Feed, and it's also saved to your Mobile Uploads album on Facebook.

✒ See Chapter 11 for more information on using the tablet's camera.

✒ The Facebook app appears on the Share menus available in other apps on the tablet. Choose that item to share on Facebook whatever it is you're looking at: a video, an image, music, and so on.

Configuring the Facebook app

Options to control the Facebook app are stored on the Settings screen, which you access by touching the More icon while viewing the main Facebook screen. (Refer to Figure 9-1 for the location of the More icon.) Choose the App Settings command.

Choose Refresh Interval to specify how frequently the app checks for new Facebook activities. If you find the one-hour value too long for your frantic Facebook social life, choose something quicker. Or, to disable Facebook automatic updates, choose Never.

To prevent videos from playing the instant you see one in the News Feed, choose the Video Auto-Play command. Choose Off to disable that feature.

Choose the Notification Ringtone item to set the sound that plays when Facebook has a new update. Choose the Silent option to mute update sounds.

Touch the Back button to close the Settings screen and return to the main Facebook screen.

All A-Twitter

Twitter is a social networking site, similar to Facebook but far briefer. On Twitter, you write short spurts of text that express your thoughts or observations, or you share links. Or you can just use Twitter to follow the thoughts and twitterings, or tweets, of other people.

✒ A message posted on Twitter is a *tweet*.

✒ A tweet can be no more than 140 characters long. That number includes spaces and punctuation.

✒ You can post messages on Twitter and follow others who post messages. Twitter is a good way to get updates and information quickly, from not only individuals but also news outlets and other organizations.

Setting up Twitter

Your Galaxy Tab most likely didn't come with the Twitter app. So your first step into the Twitterverse involves getting the app: Visit the Play Store and search for the Twitter app from Twitter, Inc. Install that app; use the directions in Chapter 15 if you need assistance.

After the Twitter app is installed, open it.

You can sign into Twitter by using your Google (Gmail) account, create an account, or use an existing account. These options are presented when the Twitter app first runs. For example, tap Create My Account to set up a new account or tap Log In to sign in with an existing account.

You may be asked whether you want the tablet to "use" your Twitter account. If you allow access, your Galaxy Tab can make Twitter posts for you, which isn't something I want, so I tapped the Cancel button.

Figure 9-4 shows the Twitter app's main screen and the current tweet feed. The Twitter app is updated frequently, so its appearance may change after this book has gone to press.

See the next section for information on *tweeting,* or updating your status using the Twitter app.

The Twitter app comes with companion widgets you can affix to the Home screen. Use the widgets to peruse recent tweets or compose a tweet. Refer to Chapter 18 for information on affixing widgets to the Home screen.

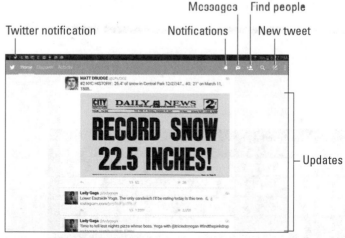

Figure 9-4: The Twitter app.

Tweeting

The Twitter app provides an excellent interface to the many wonderful and interesting things you can do with Twitter. Of course, the two most basic tasks are reading and writing tweets.

To read tweets, choose the Home category, shown in Figure 9-4. Recent tweets are displayed in a list, with the most recent information at the top. Scroll the list by swiping it with your finger. To update the list, swipe from the middle of the screen downward.

To tweet, touch the New Tweet icon (labeled to Figure 9-4). Use the New Tweet screen, shown in Figure 9-5, to compose your tweet.

Tap the Location item to add your current whereabouts to the tweet. Tap the Photo icon to add an image from the tablet's gallery.

Tap the Tweet button to share your thoughts with the Twitterverse. If you chicken out, touch the Back button and choose Discard.

- ✔ You have only 140 characters, including spaces, for creating your tweet.
- ✔ The character counter in the Twitter app lets you know how close you're getting to the 140-character limit.
- ✔ The Twitter app appears on various Share menus in other apps. You use those Share menus to send to Twitter whatever you're looking at.

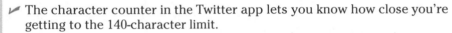

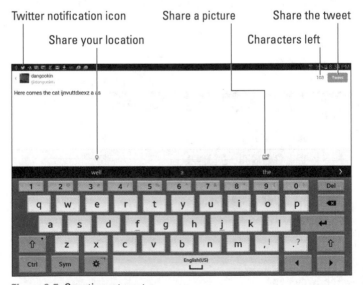

Figure 9-5: Creating a tweet.

Even More Social Networking

The Internet is nuts over social networking. Facebook may be the king, but lots of landed gentry are out for that crown. It almost seems as though a new social networking site pops up every week. Beyond Facebook and Twitter, other social networking sites include, but are not limited to

✔ Google+

✔ LinkedIn

✔ Meebo

✔ Myspace

Apps for these services are obtained from the Play Store. You can use the app itself to sign up for an account, or log in by using an existing account.

✔ See Chapter 15 for more information on the Google Play Store.

✔ Google+ is Google's social networking app, which is related to the Hangouts app. See Chapter 7 for information on using Hangouts.

✔ The HootSuite app can be used to share your thoughts on a multitude of social networking platforms

✔ As with Facebook and Twitter, you may find your social networking apps appearing on Share menus in various apps. That way, you can easily share your pictures and other types of media with your online social networking pals.

Part III
Everything in the Galaxy

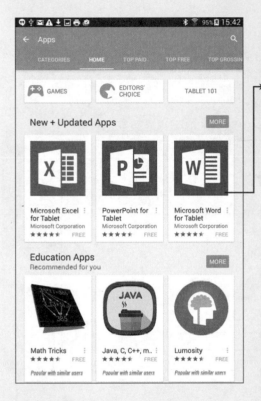 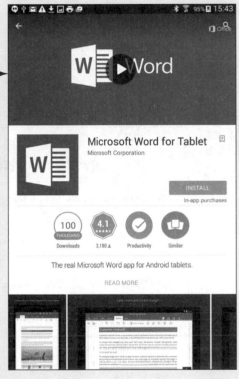

10

Getting from Here to There

In This Chapter

▶ Exploring your world with Maps

▶ Adding layers to the map

▶ Finding your location

▶ Sharing your location

▶ Searching for places

▶ Using your tablet as a navigator

▶ Creating a navigation widget

Stupid kidnappers. They took my phone but left the Galaxy Tab. I suppose they thought it might be a picture frame. Or perhaps they didn't even look inside the fine, imitation leatherette cover, figuring it was a portfolio. That was a mistake.

Even from inside the uncomfortable trunk, I could use the tablet. The screen was bright, the cellular signal was clear. The Maps app told me that I was somewhere in Seattle.

Seattle! Had they driven that far? It wasn't that important: Using the tablet, I knew not only where I was but also where a fancy Hungarian restaurant was nearby. I could send an email with my location to the authorities and then be chowing down on a hot bowl of goulash in no time. Thank heavens for the Maps app!

Budapest Bistro
4.4 ★★★★⯨ 6 reviews
Hungarian Restaurant

★ SAVE   ◉ WEBSITE   ➔ SHARE

…dway, Lynnwood, WA 98037

There's a Map for That

Your location, as well as the location of things near and far, is found on your Galaxy Tab by using the Maps app. Good news: You run no risk of improperly folding the Maps app. Better news: The Maps app charts the entire country, including freeways, highways, roads, streets, avenues, drives, bike paths, addresses, businesses, and points of interest.

Using the Maps app

You start the Maps app by choosing Maps from the Apps screen. An app launcher icon for the Maps app might also be found on the Home screen, in the Google folder.

If you're starting the app for the first time or it has been recently updated, you must agree to the terms and conditions. Do so.

The tablet communicates with global positioning system (GPS) satellites to hone in on your current location. (See the sidebar, "Activate your location!") The position is accurate to within a given range, referenced by a blue circle around your location on the map, as shown in Figure 10-1. If the circle doesn't appear, your location is either pretty darn accurate or you need to zoom in.

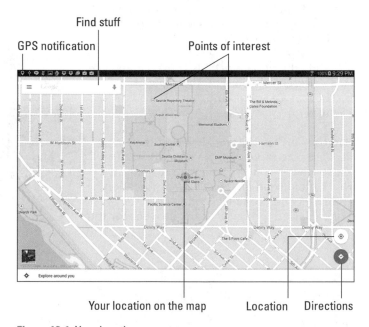

Figure 10-1: Your location on a map.

Here are some fun things you can do when viewing the map:

Zoom in: To make the map larger (to move it closer), spread your fingers on the touchscreen.

Zoom out: To make the map smaller (to see more), pinch your fingers on the touchscreen.

Pan and scroll: To see what's to the left or right or at the top or bottom of the map, drag your finger on the touchscreen; the map scrolls in the direction that you drag your finger.

 Rotate: Using two fingers, rotate the map clockwise or counterclockwise. Touch the Compass Pointer (shown in the margin) to reorient the map with north at the top of the screen.

Perspective: Touch the screen with two fingers and swipe up or down to view the map in perspective. You can also tap the Location button to switch to Perspective view, although this trick works only for your current location. To return to flat-map view, touch the Compass Pointer.

The closer you zoom in to the map, the more detail you see, such as street names, address block numbers, businesses, and other sites — but no tiny people.

- ✔ The blue triangle (barely visible in Figure 10-1) shows in which general direction the tablet is pointing.

- ✔ When the tablet's direction is unavailable, only a blue dot is shown as your location on the map.

- ✔ When all you want is a virtual compass, similar to the one you lost as a kid, get the Compass app from the Google Play Store. See Chapter 15 for more information about the Google Play Store.

Adding layers

You add details to the map by applying *layers:* A layer can enhance the map's visual appearance, provide more information, or add other fun features to the basic street map, such as Satellite view, shown in Figure 10-2.

Side menu

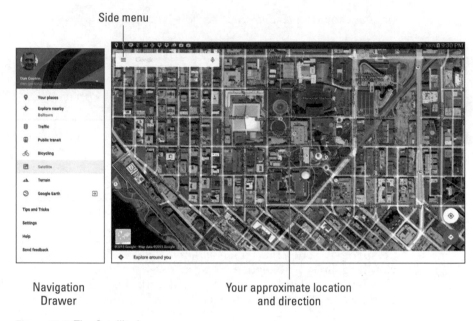

Navigation
Drawer

Your approximate location
and direction

Figure 10-2: The Satellite layer.

The key to accessing layers is to tap the Side Menu icon to view the navigation drawer. It displays several layers you can add, such as the Satellite layer shown in Figure 10-2. Another popular layer is Traffic, which lists current travel conditions.

To remove a layer, choose it again from the navigation drawer; any active layer appears highlighted. When a layer isn't applied, the Street view appears.

Activate your location!

The Maps app works best when you activate all location technology in the tablet. From the Apps screen, open the Settings icon. Tap the Connections tab. Ensure that the Master Control by the Location item is set to the On position.

The tablet uses several technologies to hone in on your location, but only when the Location setting is activated. It also uses Wi-Fi, so ensure that the Wi-Fi setting is on as well; see Chapter 16 for details on Wi-Fi. The LTE Tab also uses the mobile data network to help triangulate the tablet's current position.

It Knows Where You Are

You can look at a physical map all day long, and unless you have a sextant or a GPS, how would you know where you are? Never fear! Your tablet knows where you are. Not only does it have a GPS, but by using the Maps app, it can instantly discover where you are, find what's nearby, and even send your location to someone else.

Finding a location

The Maps app shows your location as a blue dot on the screen. But *where* is that? I mean, if you need to phone a tow truck, you can't just say, "I'm the blue dot on the orange slab by the green thing."

Well, you *can* say that, but it probably won't do any good.

To find your current street address, or any street address, long-press a location on the Maps screen. A card appears at the bottom of the screen that gives your approximate location, plus any items of interest nearby. Tap the card to view more details, as shown in Figure 10-3.

If you long-press a location, the card features additional information, including perhaps a web page address and contact info.

When you've finished viewing the card, press the Back button to return to the main Maps app screen.

✔ This location trick works only when the tablet has Internet access. When Internet access isn't available, the Maps app is unable to communicate with the Google map servers.

✔ The time under the Travel icon (the car in Figure 10-3) indicates how far away the address is from your current location. If the address is too far away, you'll see the Route icon instead, as shown in the margin.

✔ When you have *way* too much time on your hands, play with the Street View command. Choosing this option displays the location from a 360-degree perspective. In Street view, you can browse a locale, pan and tilt, or zoom in on details — whether you're familiarizing yourself with a location or planning a burglary.

Long-press a location
to see the address

Mark the location
as a favorite

Share this location

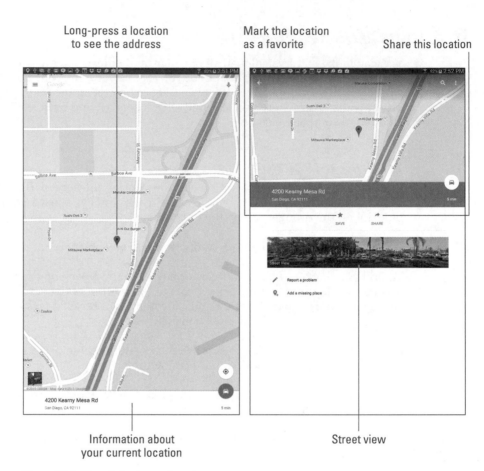

Information about
your current location

Street view

Figure 10-3: More info about a location.

Helping others find your location

It's possible to use the Maps app to send your current location to a friend. If your pal has a mobile device (phone or tablet) with smarts similar to a Galaxy Tab, he can use the coordinates to get directions to your location. Maybe he'll even bring some goulash!

To send your current location in an email message, obey these steps:

1. **Long-press your current location on the map.**

   To see your current location, tap the Location icon in the lower-right corner of the Maps app screen.

   After long-pressing your location (or any location), you see a card showing the approximate address, similar to what's shown in Figure 10-3.

2. **Tap the card, then tap the Share icon.**

3. **On the Share Via menu, choose the Gmail item.**

   The Gmail app starts, with a preset subject and message. The subject is your street address or the address of the card you touched in Step 2. The message content is the address again, but it's also a link to the current location.

4. **In the To field, type one or more recipients.**

5. **Tap the Send button to whisk off the message.**

When the recipient receives the email, he can touch the link to open your location in his Android mobile device's Maps app. When the location appears, he can follow my advice in the later section "Getting directions" for finding you. And don't loan him this book; have him buy his own copy. And bring goulash. Thanks.

Find Things

The Maps app can help you find places in the real world, just like the web browser app helps you find places on the Internet. Both operations work basically the same.

Open the Maps app and, in the Search text box, type something to find (refer to Figure 10-1). You can type a variety of terms in the Search box, as explained in this section.

Looking for a specific address

To locate an address, type it in the Search box; for example:

> 1600 Pennsylvania Ave., Washington, D.C. 20006

Tap the Search button on the keyboard, and the location is shown on the map. The next step is getting directions, which you can read about in the later section, "Getting directions."

- You don't need to type the entire address. Oftentimes, all you need is the street number and street name and then either the city name or zip code.

- As you're typing, suggestions appear below the Search box. When you see one that matches what you're looking for, tap it.

- If you omit the city name or zip code, the tablet looks for the closest matching address near your current location.

- Touch the X icon in the Search box to clear the previous search.

Finding a business, restaurant, or point of interest

You may not know an address, but you know when you crave sushi or Hungarian or perhaps the exotic flavors of Freedonia. Maybe you need a hotel or a gas station, or you have to find a place that buys old dentures. To find a business entity or a point of interest, type its name in the Search box; for example:

Movie theater

This command flags movie theaters on the current Maps screen or nearby.

To find locations near you, have the Maps app jump to your current location, as described earlier in this chapter. Otherwise, the Maps app looks for places near the area you see on the screen.

Or you can be specific and look for businesses near a certain location. Specify the city name, district, or zip code, such as

Hungarian Restaurant Seattle

After typing this command and touching the Search button, you see whatever Hungarian restaurants are found near Seattle, similar to the one shown on the left in Figure 10-4.

To see more information about a result, touch its card, such as the one for the Budapest Bistro in Figure 10-4. When more than one location is found, peruse through the list of results (cards) to see more options. After touching a card, you can view more details, similar to what's shown on the right in Figure 10-4.

 You can touch the Route button on the restaurant's (or any location's) details screen to get directions; see the later section "Getting directions."

- ✔ Spread your fingers on the touchscreen to zoom in on the map.

- ✔ Every dot on the screen represents a search result. These dots match the cards shown.

 - ✔ If you *really* like the location, touch the Favorite (star) icon. That location will be kept as one of your favorite places. The location appears as a star on the Maps app screen. See the next section.

Searching for favorite or recent places

Just as you can bookmark favorite websites on the Internet, you can mark favorite places in the real world by using the Maps app. The feature is called Saved Places.

Search text   Result   Clear search   Favorite

Result card   Directions

Figure 10-4: Finding Hungarian restaurants near Seattle, Washington.

To visit your favorite places or browse your recent map searches, tap the Side Menu icon and choose Your Places from the navigation drawer. Swipe through the list until you see the Saved Places heading. To revisit a place, tap its entry in the list.

  ✔ Mark a location as a favorite by touching the Favorite (star) icon when you view the location's details.

  ✔ Press the Back button to return to the Maps app when you've finished looking at saved places.

The Galaxy Navigator

Finding something is only half the job. The other half is getting there. Your Galaxy Tab is ever ready, thanks to the various direction and navigation features nestled in the Maps app.

✒ I don't believe that the Galaxy tablet has a car mount, at least the larger models don't. It's not a smartphone, after all. Therefore, I strongly recommend that if you use your Tab in your auto, have someone else hold it and read the directions. Or use voice navigation and, for goodness' sake, don't look at the tablet while you're driving!

✒ Navigation can consume copious amounts of power. For extra measure, plug the Tab into your car's power supply by using a micro USB car adapter. Such an adapter can be found at electronics stores and similar locations, which you can locate by using the Maps app.

Getting directions

One command associated with locations on the map is getting directions. In the Maps app, the command is called Route. Here's how to use it:

1. **Touch the Route icon in a location's card.**

   The Route icon appears as shown in the margin. When a location is found on the same screen as your current location, you may see a car icon instead. Such an icon is shown in Figure 10-3.

   After touching the Route icon, you see a screen similar to what's shown in Figure 10-5.

2. **Choose a method of transportation.**

   The available options vary, depending on your location. In Figure 10-5, the items are (from left to right) car, public transportation, on foot, and bicycle.

3. **Set a starting location.**

   You can type a location or select one of the locations shown on the screen, such as your current location, your home location, or any location you've previously searched. Touch the Starting Location item to choose another location.

4. **Ensure that the starting location and destination are what you want.**

   To reverse them, touch the Swap icon (labeled in Figure 10-5).

5. **Peruse the results.**

The map shows your route, highlighted as a blue line on the screen, as shown in Figure 10-5. Traffic jams show up as red lines, with slow traffic as yellow lines.

To see a list of directions, tap a Direction card (refer to Figure 10-5). A scrolling list appears on the screen, detailing turn-by-turn directions.

- ✔ If you don't like the route, you can adjust it: Drag the blue line by using your finger. Time and distance measurements shown on the cards change as you adjust the route.

- ✔ The Maps app alerts you to any toll roads on the specified route, as shown by the second choice in Figure 10-5. As you travel, you can choose alternative, non-toll routes if available. You're prompted to switch routes during navigation; see the next section.

- ✔ You may not get perfect directions from the Maps app, but it's a useful tool for finding places you've never visited.

Destination

Starting location

Mode of transportation

Swap   Route

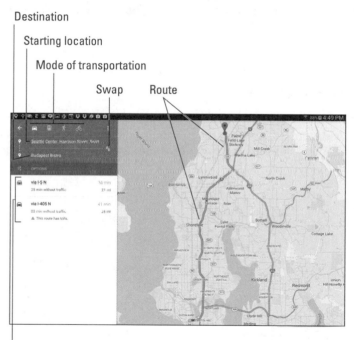

Direction cards

Figure 10-5: Planning your trip.

Adding a navigation Home screen widget

When you visit certain places often — such as the liquor store or your parole office — you can save yourself the time you would spend repeatedly inputting navigation information. All you need to do is create a navigation widget on the Home screen. Here's how:

1. **On the Galaxy Tab S, long-press the Home screen and then tap the Widgets icon; on the Tab 4, tap the Apps icon and then the Widgets tab on the Apps screen.**

2. **Long-press the Directions widget and drag it to a spot on the Home screen.**

   See Chapter 18 for complete information on adding widgets to the Home screen.

3. **Choose a traveling method.**

   Your options are by car, by public transportation, on foot, or by bicycle.

4. **In the Choose Destination text box, type a destination, a contact name, an address, or a business.**

5. **Type a shortcut name.**

   The name appears below the icon on the Home screen.

6. **Tap the Save button.**

   The widget is affixed to the Home screen.

Tap the widget to use it. Instantly, the Maps app starts and enters Navigation mode, steering you from wherever you are to the location referenced in Step 4.

It's a Big, Flat Camera

In This Chapter

▶ Taking a picture

▶ Recording video

▶ Shooting a panorama

▶ Capturing the screen

▶ Deleting the image you just shot

▶ Turning on the flash

▶ Changing the resolution

Cameras have come a long way since Nicéphore Niépce took a daylong exposure of his backyard using a *camera obscura*. Photography was an analog, real-world thing until the 1990s. Then technology went digital. In a few more years, no one will be around who remembers what a roll of film was.

What's also changed is the camera. No longer do you hold the thing up to your face. Instead, you hold the device at arm's length and peer at an LCD screen. What's even stranger is holding up a large, flat object such as the Galaxy Tab and using it to take a picture. Sure, it works. It's handy. But it's just unusual and different enough that I present to you an entire chapter on using your tablet as a camera.

Your Galactic Camera

I admit that a Samsung Galaxy Tab isn't the world's best camera. And I'm sure that Mr. Spock's tricorder wasn't the best camera in the *Star Trek* universe, either. That comparison is kind of the whole point: Your tablet is an incredible gizmo that does many things. Two of those things are taking pictures and recording video, as described in this section.

Introducing the Camera app

Both picture-taking and video-recording duties on your Galaxy Tab are handled by the same app, the Camera app. You may be able to find a shortcut to that app on the Home screen, and it also dwells with all its app buddies on the Apps screen.

The Camera app controls both the main camera, which is on the tablet's backside, and the front-facing camera, which is not on the tablet's backside.

After starting the Camera app on the Galaxy Tab S, you see the main Camera screen, as illustrated in Figure 11-1. The Galaxy Tab 4's version of the Camera app is shown in Figure 11-2. Both apps offer similar features, just not in the same location.

The tablet's touchscreen serves as the viewfinder; what you see on the screen is exactly what appears in the final photo or video.

✔ The tablet can be used as a camera in either landscape or portrait orientation.

✔ The main (rear) camera focuses automatically. To override the automatic focus on the Galaxy Tab S, tap the screen to move the focus ring and bring a certain part of the image into focus.

✔ Zoom in by spreading your fingers on the screen.

✔ Zoom out by pinching your fingers on the screen.

✔ The Tab 4 also uses the Volume button to zoom in or out: Up volume zooms in, and down volume zooms out.

✔ You can take as many pictures or record as much video with your tablet as you like, as long as you don't run out of space in the tablet's internal storage or external storage. Speaking of which:

✔ A microSD icon on the screen (shown in Figures 11-1 and 11-2) indicates that images and recordings are saved to the tablet's microSD card. When a microSD card isn't installed, images are stored on the tablet's internal storage.

✔ If your pictures or videos appear blurry, ensure that the camera lens on the back of the tablet isn't dirty. Or perhaps you may have neglected to remove the plastic cover from the rear camera when you first set up your Tab.

✔ See Chapter 12 for information on previewing and managing pictures and videos.

Shortcut area

Switch camera

MicroSD card icon

Shutter

Record video

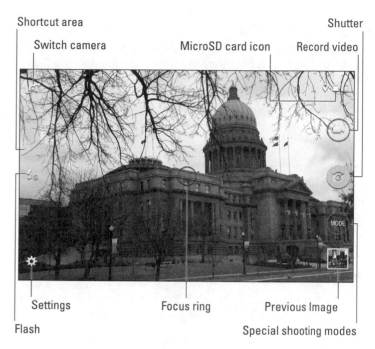

Settings

Focus ring

Previous Image

Flash

Special shooting modes

Figure 11-1: The Galaxy Tab S Camera app.

Settings

Switch camera

MicroSD card icon

Shutter

Still/Video modes

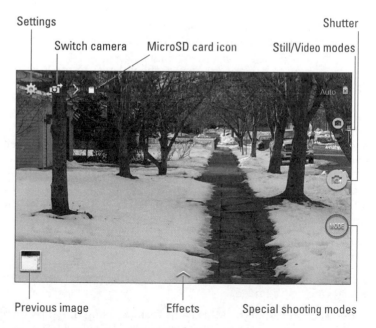

Previous image

Effects

Special shooting modes

Figure 11-2: The Galaxy Tab 4 Camera app.

Taking a still image

To take a still picture, tap the Shutter icon, shown in the margin. The camera focuses, you may hear a mechanical shutter sound, and the flash may go off. You're ready to take the next picture.

To preview the image, touch the Previous Image thumbnail (labeled in Figures 11-1 and 11-2. After viewing the preview, press the Back button to return to the Camera app.

✔ Set the image's resolution before you shoot. See the later section, "Changing the resolution."

✔ The Galaxy Tab stores pictures in the JPEG image file format, using the .jpg filename extension. The images are stored in the DCIM/Camera folder in either internal storage or on the microSD card.

Recording video

To record video on the Galaxy Tab S, tap the Video icon, shown in the margin. The icon disappears, and you'll find a Stop and Pause icon on the screen.

On the Galaxy Tab 4, choose Video mode (refer to Figure 11-2) by sliding the Still/Video button to the Video position. Tap the Record icon, shown in the margin, to begin recording.

While recording, *REC* (recording) appears in the upper-left corner of the screen. You also see a time index and storage information.

Tap the Pause icon to temporarily pause the video. Tap the Record (red dot) icon again to continue the same recording.

Tap the Stop icon when you've finished recording.

Preview the video by tapping the Previous Image icon on the Camera app's screen.

✔ Hold the tablet steady when recording video! The camera still works when you whip the tablet around, but wild gyrations render the video unwatchable.

✔ Set video quality before recording video. See the section, "Setting video quality," later in this chapter.

✔ While recording on the Galaxy Tab S, you can press the Volume button to capture a still image.

✔ Videos are stored in the MPEG4 file format, using the .mp4 filename extension. You'll find the videos in the DCIM/Camera folder, either in internal storage or on the microSD card.

Doing a selfie

Who needs to pay all that money for a mirror when you have the Galaxy Tab? You can forget the mirror. Instead, think about taking all those selfies without having to second-guess whether the camera is pointed at your face.

To take your own mug shot, follow these steps:

1. **Start the Camera app.**

2. **Tap the Switch Camera icon.**

   When you see yourself on the screen, you're doing it properly.

3. **Snap a still image or record a video.**

   Refer to directions earlier in this chapter for details.

Touch the Switch Camera icon again to direct the Galaxy Tab to use the main (rear) camera.

Taking in a panorama

No, a *panorama* isn't an exotic new alcoholic drink; it's a wide shot, like a landscape, a beautiful vista, or a family photograph after a garlic feast. To take a panoramic shot using your Galaxy Tab, switch the camera to Panorama mode. Obey these steps:

1. **Start the Camera app.**

2. **Tab the Mode button.**

   The Mode button appears only when the Tab 4 Camera app is in single-shot mode.

   An extensive list of shooting modes appears on the screen. Swipe the list to peruse the variety.

3. **Choose Panorama.**

   Directions for capturing a panorama may appear on the screen. Tap the OK button to dismiss.

4. **Hold your arms steady.**

5. **Tap the Shutter icon.**

   You see a frame and a guide on the screen, which approximates the current shot and the extent (left-right or up-down) for the panorama. Arrows point in the directions in which you can pan.

6. **Pivot slightly to your right (or in another direction, but you must continue in the same direction).**

As you move the camera, the onscreen frame adjusts to your new position. Watch the progress bar on the screen to help keep the panorama even. All you need to do is keep moving.

7. **Continue pivoting as subsequent shots are taken, or tap the Shutter icon again to finish the panorama.**

After the last image is snapped, wait while the panorama is assembled.

The Camera app sticks the different shots together, creating a panoramic image.

It's important that you exit Panorama mode when you're finished. To return the Camera app to normal still-shooting image mode, tap the Mode button and choose Auto.

See the later section, "Using modes and adding effects," for more details on various shooting modes and effects available in the Camera app.

Deleting something you just shot

Disappointed with that image or video? Perhaps someone you love is hanging over your shoulder weeping and begging you to remove it. Hastily follow these steps:

1. **Tap the Previous Image thumbnail that appears on the Camera app's screen (refer to Figures 11-1 and 11-2).**

After touching the preview, you see the full-screen image. Videos appear with a Play icon center screen.

2. **Tap the Delete (trash can) icon.**

If you don't see the trash can icon, tap the screen and it shows up.

3. **Tap the Delete or OK button to confirm.**

4. **Press the Back button to return to the Camera app.**

When you desire destruction of more than just the last image you took (or video you recorded), visit the Gallery app. See Chapter 12.

Capturing the screen

A *screen shot,* also called a *screen cap* (for capture), is a picture of your tablet's touchscreen. So if you see something interesting on the screen, or just want to take a quick pic of your tablet life, you take a screen shot.

To capture the screen, hold your hand perpendicular to the tablet, like you're giving it a karate chop. Swipe the edge of your palm over the screen, right-to-left or left-to-right. Upon success, you'll hear a shutter sound.

Upon failure, confirm that this feature is enabled. Heed these directions:

1. **Open the Settings app.**
2. **On the Tab S, tap the Device tab; on the Tab 4, tap the Controls tab.**
3. **On the left side of the screen, choose Motions or Palm Motion.**
4. **Ensure that the item Palm Swipe to Capture (Tab S) or Capture Screen (Tab 4) is active.**

   If not, tap the Master Control on the right so that it's green, or in the on position.

Likewise, to disable this feature — because you frequently karate-chop your tablet and don't like all the accumulated screen shots — slide the Master Control to the Off position in Step 4.

 ✔ As a bonus, the captured screen is saved to the Clipboard, where you can paste it into an app that accepts graphic input. See Chapter 4 for information on cut, copy, and paste.

 ✔ You can view the screen shots by using the Gallery app. You'll find them in the Screenshots album. See Chapter 12 for information on the Gallery app.

 ✔ Screen shots are kept in the Pictures/Screenshots folder in the tablet's internal storage. They're saved in the PNG graphics file format.

Camera Settings and Options

The Camera app sports multiple features, some of which you'll probably never use. It's good to have variety, but without some advice, it's difficult to know which features are important and which you can play with later. This section lists many of the important features and options.

Setting the flash

Not all Galaxy Tabs feature a flash on the rear camera. If your tablet does, you can set the flash's behavior by tapping the Flash icon on the app's main screen, shown in Figure 11-1. The three flash modes are described in Table 11-1, along with the icons representing each mode.

Table 11-1		Galaxy Tablet Camera Flash Settings
Setting	**Icon**	**Description**
Auto	⚡A	The flash activates during low-light situations but not when it's bright out.
On	⚡	The flash always activates.
Off	⚡⊘	The flash never activates, even in low-light situations.

Tap the Flash icon to cycle between flash modes.

✔ If you don't see the Flash icon, tap the Settings icon on the Camera app's main screen. Tap the Flash item to cycle through the modes.

✔ When recording video, the tablet's flash lamp is either on or off. Choose the Flash On icon before shooting to enable the lamp.

✔ A good time to turn on the flash is when taking pictures of people or objects in front of something bright, such as a fuzzy brown kitten playing with a ball of white yarn in front of an exploding gasoline truck.

Changing the resolution

Too many people ignore the image resolution setting, not only on tablets but on digital cameras as well. Either that, or they just figure that the highest resolution is the best resolution. That's not always the case.

Customizing the shortcut area

You can customize the icons that appear on the left side of the Camera app's screen on the Galaxy Tab S. In Figure 11-1, the Flash icon is shown. Room is available for more icons. To add them, tap the Settings icon, and then drag one of the squares to the left edge of the screen. These icons provide quick access to camera features you use frequently.

To remove a shortcut, tap the Settings icon, and then drag the shortcut from the left side of the screen back into the grid. Room is available for up to three shortcuts; if you add more, an existing icon is replaced.

High-resolution is ideal for printing pictures and for photo editing. It's not ideal for images you plan on sharing with Facebook or sending as an email attachment. Further, the higher the resolution, the more storage space each image consumes. Don't be disappointed when your tablet fills up with vacation photos because the resolution is too high.

Another problem with resolution is remembering to set it *before* you snap the photo. Here's what to do in the Camera app to set image resolution:

1. **Tap the Settings icon.**
2. **On the Tab 4, ensure that the Camera tab is chosen.**
3. **Choose the Picture Size item or the Photo Size item.**
4. **Select a resolution from those listed.**

    Resolutions are listed by megapixels, horizontal and vertical dimensions, and then form factor. The form factor is 4:3 for a traditional image, 16:9 for widescreen, and 1:1 for square.

5. **Press the Back button to dismiss the Settings grid.**

    All the images taken are captured at the new resolution.

The tablet's front-facing camera has different resolutions than the rear camera. You must first switch to the front camera to set its resolution.

Megapixel is a measurement of the amount of information stored in an image. A megapixel is approximately 1 million *pixels,* or individual dots that compose an image.

Setting video quality

To set the resolution for recording video, work through the same steps presented in the preceding section. For the Tab 4, choose the Video tab in Step 2. In Step 3, choose Video Size.

Video quality is presented as Full HD, HD, or VGA, ranking in quality from best to not-as-best. Aspect ratio is shown with 16:9 as widescreen and 4:3 as standard video.

Set the video quality before you shoot!

Activating the location tag

Your Galactic tablet's camera not only takes a picture but also keeps track of where you're located on planet earth when you take the picture. The feature is commonly called Geo-Tag, but in the Camera app it's known as Location Tag.

To ensure that the Geo-Tag feature is enabled, or to disable the feature, carefully follow these steps:

1. **Tap the Settings icon in the Camera app.**

2. **On the Tab 4, tap the Settings icon tab.**

3. **Look at the Location Tag item.**

   The text *On* or *Off* appears, indicating whether the feature is on or off.

4. **Switch the feature on or off.**

   The first time you set this item, you may see descriptive text explaining what it does. Tap the OK button.

 When the Location Tag feature is activated, the Location icon appears on the Camera's screen. The icon is shown in the margin.

See Chapter 12 for information on perusing a photograph's location. Also included in that chapter is information on removing a photo's location information.

Using modes and adding effects

Two items you can adjust in the Camera app are the shooting mode and visual effects. These are optional adjustments and it's perfectly okay to use the Camera app without bothering with either feature.

Shooting modes are handled by the Mode button (labeled in Figures 11-1 and 11-2). The modes appear, lined up on the screen; swipe them to view the lot. Choose one to experiment with it; descriptive information appears explaining what the mode does and how it works.

On the Tab S camera app, visual effects are chosen by tapping the Settings icon and choosing Effects. For the Tab 4, tap the Effects chevron at the bottom of the screen. Tap a square to witness how the effect changes what you see in the viewfinder.

✔ The standard shooting mode is Auto. Don't forget to switch back to that mode when you've finished playing with the other modes.

✔ To remove visual effects, choose No Effect from the list.

✔ Additional shooting modes and visual effects can be obtained for the Galaxy Tab S by choosing the Download item. Some of the modes and effects are free, but a few must be purchased.

12

The Gallery

In This Chapter

▶ Viewing images and videos

▶ Finding an image's location

▶ Setting an image as wallpaper

▶ Editing images

▶ Deleting pictures and videos

▶ Saving pictures to the Internet

▶ Publishing a video on YouTube

▶ Sharing images and videos

There's no point in the Galaxy Tab having a camera unless it also has a place to store pictures and videos. That location is a digital Louvre of sorts called the Gallery. It's more than just a point-at-the-Picasso type of gallery because, in addition to looking at the painting of the woman with the weird eyeballs, you can use the Gallery app to fix those eyes. Or you can accept the eyeballs and flip to the next photo. The Gallery app does it all.

Your Pictures and Videos

Some people hang their pictures on the wall. Some put pictures on a piano or maybe on a mantle. In the digital realm, pictures are stored electronically, compressed and squeezed into a series of ones and zeroes that means nothing unless you have an app that lets you view those images. On your Galactic tablet, that app is the *Gallery*.

 Google strongly suggests that you use the Photos app instead of the Gallery. My advice is to stick with the Gallery as long as it's available on your Tab. The Photos app also displays images and videos, and it offers more editing tools, but it's not as easy to understand or use.

Visiting the Gallery

Start the Gallery app by choosing its icon from the Apps screen, or you may find a Gallery launcher icon lurking on the Home screen. When the Gallery app opens, you see pictures organized into albums, similar to what's shown in Figure 12-1.

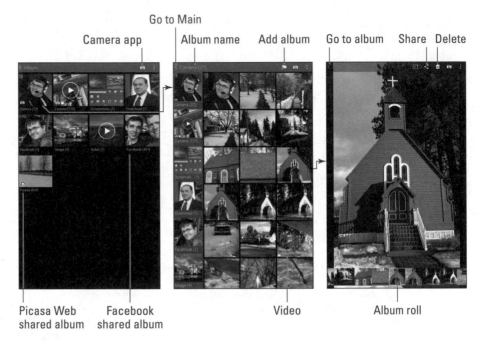

Go to Main

Camera app   Album name   Add album   Go to album   Share   Delete

Picasa Web   Facebook   Video   Album roll
shared album   shared album

Figure 12-1: The Gallery app.

TIP

If you see the Camera app when you start the Gallery, press the Back button to return to the Gallery. (The Camera and Gallery apps are linked and sometimes one starts instead of the other.)

The number and variety of albums (refer to Figure 12-1) depend on how you synchronize your Tab with your computer, which apps you use for collecting media, and which photo-sharing services you use on the Internet and have synchronized with the tablet.

Tap an album to display that album's contents; the pictures appear in a grid of thumbnail previews. Swipe the screen left and right to peruse them all.

Touch an individual thumbnail in the album to view that item full size on the screen, similar to what's shown in Figure 12-1, right. You can rotate the tablet horizontally (or vertically) to see the image in another orientation. Spread your fingers or pinch on the touchscreen to zoom in or out, respectively. Swipe the screen to page through images in an album.

If any videos are stored in an album, they appear with a Play icon. Tap that icon to view the video. (You may be prompted to choose an app; select the Video Player and then tap Always.) As the video is playing, touch the screen again to see the control to pause the video.

 You back up from an image or a video to an album by pressing the Back button. Press the button again to return to the main Gallery screen.

> ✔ The Galaxy Tab 4's Gallery app looks subtly different from what's shown in Figure 12-1. Categories are chosen from an action bar in the upper-left corner of the main screen, unlike Figure 12-1, which uses a Side Menu icon.

> ✔ The Camera album contains pictures you've shot using the tablet's camera.

> ✔ If you see two Camera albums, as shown in Figure 12-1, one represents images on the device and the other on external storage (the microSD card).

> ✔ The Download album contains images downloaded from the Internet.

> ✔ Albums labeled with special icons, such as the Picasa Web and Facebook icons shown in Figure 12-1, have been synchronized between your tablet and the Internet.

> ✔ Various apps may also create their own albums in the Gallery app.

> ✔ Touch an image (far right in Figure 12-1) to see the onscreen controls and other information.

> ✔ To view all the images in an album, tap the Action Overflow icon and choose Slideshow. Playing a slide show turns your expensive tablet into a less-expensive digital picture frame.

> ✔ Refer to Chapter 19 for information on using a photo from the Gallery as the tablet's Home screen or Lock screen wallpaper.

Finding a picture's location

Your tablet can be configured to save additional information with each picture you snap. Details are offered in Chapter 11. What you can do with that information is display it while viewing a picture, and even locate the exact spot where you took a picture, right on the Maps app.

To view location information for a photo in the Gallery app, heed these steps:

1. Display the image full-screen.

Refer to the preceding section for details.

2. **Tap the Action Overflow icon.**

   If you don't see the icon, tap the screen and it shows up.

3. **Choose the command More Info (Tab S) or Details (Tab 4).**

   You see information stored with the video, including the date, location, and other trivia. The Tab S version is similar to what's shown in Figure 12-2.

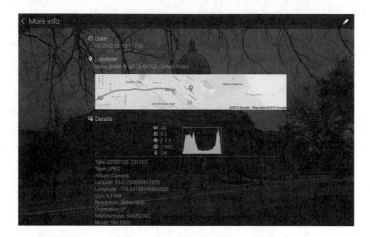

Figure 12-2: Image location and other information.

Tap the map preview (refer to Figure 12-2) to visit the location by using a Maps app-like preview. (It's not really the Maps app, which is covered in Chapter 10.)

The location information stays with the image, even if you share the photo on the Internet. To remove the information, tap the Edit (pencil) icon (upper-right corner, shown in Figure 12-2), and then tap the minus sign next to the location information. Tap the Done button and the data is removed.

↳ The Tab 4's Gallery app doesn't display location information as shown in Figure 12-2. It's also not possible to edit the information.

↳ Not every image stores location information. In some cases, the tablet cannot read its GPS radio to store the information. Other times, the feature is disabled. When this happens, location information is unavailable.

↳ Refer to Chapter 11 for information on how to turn location information on or off when taking pictures.

Photo and Video Editing

The best tool for image editing is a computer armed with photo-editing software, such as Photoshop or one of its less expensive alternatives. Even so, it's possible to use the Gallery app to perform some minor photo surgery. This section highlights some of the more useful things you can do.

Cropping a picture

One of the true image-editing commands available in the Gallery app is Crop. You can use Crop to slice out portions of an image, such as when removing ex-spouses and convicts from a family portrait. To crop an image, obey these directions when using the Gallery app:

1. **Summon the image you want to crop.**

2. **Tap the Action Overflow icon and choose the Crop command.**

   If the Crop command is unavailable, you have to choose another image; not every image in the Gallery can be modified. (Specifically, you can't edit images brought in from social networking sites.)

3. **Work the crop thing.**

   You can drag the rectangle around to choose which part of the image to crop. Drag an edge of the rectangle to resize the left and right or top and bottom sides. Or drag a corner of the rectangle to change the rectangle's size proportionally. Use Figure 12-3 as your guide.

4. **Tap the Done button when you've finished cropping.**

   Only the portion of the image within the rectangle is saved, the rest is discarded.

The cropped image is saved as a new picture in the Gallery. So if you don't like the crop, delete the cropped image and start over again with the original. See the later section "Deleting pictures and videos" for image destruction details.

Trimming a video

The process of *trimming* a video involves snipping off the head or tail from the recording. It works like this:

1. **Display the video in the Gallery.**

   Do not play the video; just have it loitering on the screen.

Portion kept   Portion discarded

Drag rectangle   Adjust sides and corners

Figure 12-3: Working the crop-thing.

2. Tap the Trim icon.

The icon looks like a pair of scissors, similar to what's shown in the margin. If you can't see the icon, touch the screen. If it still doesn't show up, the video is being shared from another source and cannot be edited.

3. Adjust the video's start and end points.

Figure 12-4 illustrates how to trim a typical video: Adjust the Start and End markers to trim the video's length. Touch the Play button on the screen to preview how the shortened video looks. Adjust the Start and End markers further, if needed.

You cannot trim a video so that it's less than one second in duration.

4. Tap the Done button to save the edited video.

An Enter New File Name box appears.

5. Type a new name for the video or edit the existing name.

6. Touch the OK button.

The trimmed video is saved under the new name specified in Step 5.

The original video is not altered by trimming; instead a new video is created.

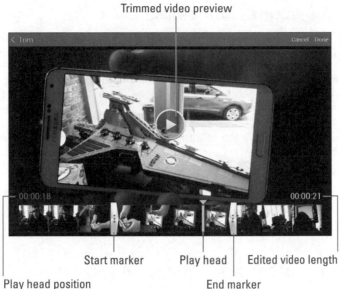

Figure 12-4: Film Editing 101.

Rotating pictures

Which way is up? Well, the answer depends on your situation. For taking pictures with your Tab, sometimes images just don't appear up, no matter how you turn the screen. To remedy that situation, heed these steps:

1. **Choose an image to rotate.**

   Display the image on a screen by itself, as described earlier in this chapter.

2. **Tap the Action Overflow icon.**

   Tap the screen to summon the onscreen controls should they vanish.

3. **Choose Rotate Left to rotate the image counterclockwise; choose Rotate Right to rotate the image clockwise.**

You can rotate a slew of images at one time: Select all the images as described in the later section "Selecting multiple pictures and videos." Then tap the Action Overflow icon and choose Rotate Left or Rotate Right. All the images are rotated at once.

✔ You cannot rotate videos.

✔ You cannot rotate certain images, such as images shared from your Picasa Web albums.

Deleting pictures and videos

It's entirely possible, and often desirable, to remove unwanted, embarrassing, or questionably legal images and videos from the Gallery.

 To zap a single image or a video, summon the image or video and touch the trash can icon that appears atop the screen. Touch the Delete or OK button to confirm. It's gone.

✔ You can delete a swath of images by selecting a group at a time. See the next section.

 ✔ You can't undelete an image or a video you've deleted. There's no way to recover such an image using available tools on your Galaxy Tab.

✔ Some images can't be edited, such as images brought in from social networking sites or from online photo-sharing albums.

Selecting multiple pictures and videos

You can apply certain commands, such as Delete and Rotate, to an entire collection of items in the Gallery at once. To do so, you must select a group of images or videos. Here's how:

1. **Open the album you want to mess with.**

2. **Long-press an item to select it.**

   Instantly, you activate image selection mode. (That's my name for it.) The screen changes to look like Figure 12-5.

3. **Tap additional images and videos to select them.**

   Or you can choose Select All from the action bar (labeled in Figure 12-5).

4. **Perform an action on the group of images or videos.**

   To remove the images, tap the Delete icon. To share the images with other sources, tap the Share icon. (Both icons are labeled in Figure 12-5.) If you tap the Action Overflow icon, you'll see actions that apply to the group.

To deselect items, touch them again. To deselect everything, choose Unselect All from the action bar. Or if you want to cancel deselecting items, tap the left-pointing chevron in the upper-left corner of the screen.

The type of commands you can use on a group of items in an album depends on the group. Some commands, such as Delete and Share, can be performed on any old group. Other commands, such as the image rotation commands, work only with pictures, not videos.

Cancel selection

Selection action bar   Share   Delete

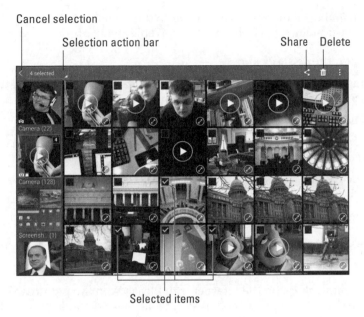

Selected items

Figure 12-5: Choosing images to mess with.

Set Your Pics and Vids Free

Keeping your precious moments and memories by themselves in the Tab
is an elegant solution to the problem of lugging around photo albums and a
video projector. When you want to show your pictures to the widest possible
audience, you need a bigger stage. That stage is the Internet, and you have
many ways to send and save your pictures and videos online, as covered in
this section.

- ✏ Refer to Chapter 17 for information on synchronizing and sharing
  information between the Galaxy Tab and a computer.
- ✏ Refer to Chapter 17 also for information on printing pictures on
  your Tab.

Accessing your Picasa Web account

Part of your Google account includes access to Picasa Web, the online
photo-sharing website. If you haven't yet been to the Picasa Web site on the
Internet, use your computer to visit http://picasaweb.google.com.

Configure things by logging into your Google account on that website.

The Picasa Web account should be synchronized and configured automatically with your Galaxy Tab. So if you've saved pictures on the Picasa Web site,

you can find them on the tablet, similar to those shown in Figure 12-1. If not, follow these steps to ensure that Picasa Web is being property synced:

1. **Open the Settings app.**

2. **Tap the General tab and choose Accounts on the left side of the screen.**

3. **Choose your Google account on the right side of the screen.**

4. **Tap your Gmail account under the Accounts heading on the Google screen.**

5. **Ensure that there's a check mark by the item Sync Picasa Web Albums.**

   That's pretty much it.

Any images you have on Picasa Web are automatically copied to your Galaxy Tab from now on.

If you want to share on the Internet with Picasa Web the pictures you take with the Camera app, you need to select and share the images. See the later section "Sharing images with other apps."

✔ Picasa Web albums feature the Picasa Web logo, as shown in the margin.

✔ Images copied from your Picasa Web account to the Tab cannot be edited or deleted. You might find other restrictions on the images.

✔ The best way to manage Picasa Web images is to go to the Picasa Web site on the Internet.

Uploading to Dropbox

Another way to share images on the Internet is to use your Dropbox account. As this book goes to press, the Dropbox app is included with your Galaxy Tab, and signing up for Dropbox is part of the tablet's setup and configuration. Even if that's no longer the case, you can still obtain and use Dropbox to save and share photos. In fact, sharing photos is automatic. Obey these steps:

1. **Open the Dropbox app.**

2. **Tap the Action Overflow icon and choose Settings.**

3. **Tap the item Turn On Camera Upload.**

   If the item instead reads Turn Off Camera Upload, you're all set. Unless you have an LTE Tab, in which case I recommend that you:

4. **Select the Upload Using item, and then choose Wi-Fi Only.**

   By setting this item, you ensure that the tablet uploads images only when connected to a Wi-Fi network. That means you won't subtract precious megabytes from your monthly mobile data allocation.

With camera upload on, any image you snap is instantly copied to the Camera Uploads folder in your Dropbox account. If you use Dropbox on a computer, you can immediately access those pictures and videos. That's handy.

Posting a video to YouTube

The best way to share a video is to upload it to YouTube. As a Google account holder, you also have a YouTube account. You can use the tablet's YouTube app to upload your videos to the Internet, where everyone can see them and make rude comments. Here's how:

1. **Ensure that the Wi-Fi connection is activated.**

   The best way to upload a video is to turn on the Wi-Fi connection, which doesn't incur data surcharges like the digital cellular network does.

2. **Open the Gallery app.**

3. **Choose the video you want to upload.**

   You do not need to play the video. Just have it on the screen.

 4. **Tap the Share icon.**

   If you don't see the Share icon, tap the screen.

5. **Choose YouTube.**

6. **If prompted, choose your Google/Gmail account and tap OK.**

7. **Type the video's title.**

8. **Type a description.**

   The description appears on YouTube when people go to view the video.

9. **Set whether the video is private, public, or unlisted.**

   A private video is viewable only by you or anyone you specifically invite to view it. A public video is viewable by everyone in the universe. An unlisted video is viewable by anyone to whom you share the video's link; it cannot be searched for in YouTube.

10. **Tap the Upload button.**

    You return to the gallery, and the video is uploaded. The video continues to upload even if the tablet falls asleep.

The uploading notification appears while the video is being sent to YouTube. When the upload has completed, the notification stops animating and becomes the Video Uploaded Successfully icon, as shown in the margin.

To view your video, open the YouTube app. It's found on the Apps screen and discussed in detail in Chapter 14.

- YouTube often takes awhile to process a video after it's uploaded. Allow a few minutes to pass (longer for larger videos) before expecting the video to be available for viewing.

- *Upload* is the official term to describe sending a file from the Galaxy Tab to the Internet.

Sharing images with other apps

 Just about every app wants to get in on the sharing bit, especially when it comes to sharing pictures and videos. The key is to view something in the Gallery and then tap the Share icon atop the screen (and shown in the margin). From the Share menu, choose an app and that image or video is instantly sent to that app.

What happens next?

That depends on the app. For Facebook, Twitter, and other social networking apps, the image is attached to a new post. For Email or Gmail, the image or video becomes an attachment. Other apps treat the image in a similar manner: It's made available to the app for sharing, posting, sending, or what have you. The key is to look for that Share icon.

13

Music, Music, Music

In This Chapter

▶ Finding music on the Tab

▶ Enjoying a tune

▶ Turning the tablet into a deejay

▶ Transferring music from your computer

▶ Organizing your tunes into a playlist

▶ Listening to streaming music

Your tablet's amazing arsenal of features includes its capability to play music. So it effectively replaces any gramophone that you've been lugging around, which is the whole idea behind such an all-in-one gizmo like a Galaxy Tab. You can cheerfully and adeptly transfer all your old Edison cylinders and 78 LPs over to the tablet for your listening enjoyment. This chapter tells you how.

Your Hit Parade

The source of your musical joy on the Galaxy tablet is an app aptly named Play Music. You can find that app on the Apps screen. It might also dwell inside the Google folder on the Home screen.

✔ The first time you start the Play Music app, you may be asked whether you'd like to try Google Play Music All Access. It's an all-the-time music service from Google, available for a monthly fee. You do not have to subscribe to the service to use the Play Music app on your tablet.

✔ The Galaxy Tab also comes with a Samsung app called Music. It offers the same features as Play Music and works similarly.

Browsing your music library

The Play Music app lists music available on your tablet as well as music associated with your online Google account. To view your music library, obey these steps:

1. **Start the Play Music app.**

2. **Tap the Side Menu icon to display the navigation drawer.**

   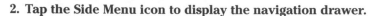

   The Side Menu icon is found in the upper-left corner of the screen. It's shown in the margin. If you see a left-pointing arrow instead, tap that arrow until the icon appears.

3. **Choose My Library.**

The Play Music app is shown in Figure 13-1 with the My Library screen selected. Your music is organized by categories, which appear as tabs atop the screen. Switch categories by tapping a tab, or swipe the screen left or right to browse your music library.

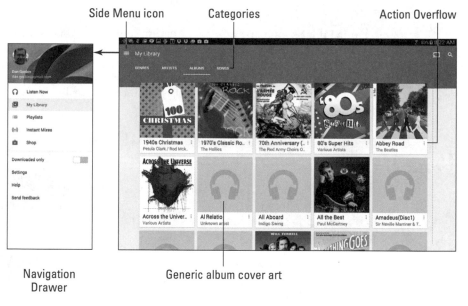

Side Menu icon   Categories   Action Overflow

Navigation Drawer

Generic album cover art

Figure 13-1: The Music library.

The categories are merely ways the music is organized — ways to make the music easier to find when you may know, say, an artist's name but not an album title. The Genres category is for those times when you're in the mood for a certain type of music but don't know, or don't mind, who recorded it.

- Pay attention to the wee Action Overflow icon. You'll find it affixed to albums, as shown in Figure 13-1, and also songs. Use this icon to control your music, as described elsewhere in this chapter.

- Two types of album artwork are used by the Play Music app. For purchased music, or music recognized by the app, original album artwork appears. Otherwise, the app shows a generic album cover.

- When the tablet can't recognize an artist, it uses the title Unknown Artist. This usually happens with music you copy manually to your tablet, but it can also apply to audio recordings you make.

Playing a tune

After perusing your music library, select a tune to play it. If you tap a song, it plays. When you tap on an album, you'll see the list of individual songs, plus a large Play icon, shown in the margin. Tap that icon to listen to the entire album.

When the song plays, controls and other information appear at the bottom of the screen, as shown in Figure 13-2. Tap that strip to view full-screen controls.

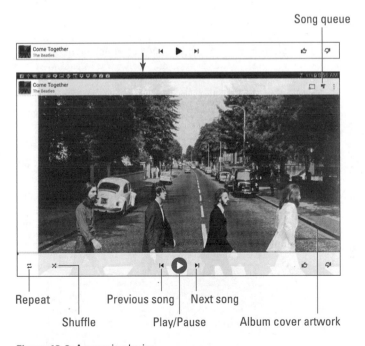

Figure 13-2: A song is playing.

You're free to do other things while music plays on your Tab. You can even lock the screen and the music plays. Choose the Play Music notification, shown in the margin, to return to the Play Music app. While using the tablet, pull down the notifications panel and use the controls on the Play Music notification to pause the music or skip to the next or previous song.

After the song has finished playing, the next song in the list plays. The list order depends on how you start the song. For example, if you start a song from the album view, all songs in that album play in the order listed.

The next song in the list doesn't play if you have the Shuffle button activated (refer to Figure 13-2). In that case, the Play Music app randomly chooses another song from the same list. Who knows which one will be next?

The next song might not play also when you have the Repeat option on: The three Repeat settings, as well as the Shuffle settings, are listed in Table 13-1. To change settings, tap the Shuffle icon or the Repeat icon.

Table 13-1		Shuffle and Repeat Icons
Icon	*Setting*	*What Happens When You Touch the Icon*
⤬	No Shuffle	Songs play one after the other.
⤬	Shuffle	Songs are played in random order.
⟲	No Repeat	Songs don't repeat.
⟲₁	Single Repeat	The same song plays over and over.
⟲	List Repeat	All songs in the list play over and over.

To stop a song from playing, tap the Play/Pause icon.

- ✔ You set the volume by using the tablet's Volume button.

- ✔ To change the song order, tap the Song Queue icon, shown in Figure 13-2. You see a list of song cards in the order the songs play. Use the tab on the left of each song card to change the order; drag the card up or down. Also see the section, "Organize Your Music," later in this chapter.

- ✔ You can use the Galaxy tablet's search capabilities to help locate tunes in your Music library. You can search by artist name, song title, or album. The key is to touch the Search icon when you're using the Play Music app. Type all or part of the text you're searching for, and then touch the Search button on the onscreen keyboard. Choose the song you want to hear from the list that's displayed.

"What's this song?"

You might consider getting a handy, music-oriented widget called Sound Search for Google Play. You can obtain it from the Google Play Store and then add it to the Home screen, as described in Chapter 18. From the Home screen, you can use the widget to identify music playing within earshot of your tablet.

To use the widget, touch it on the Home screen. The widget immediately starts listening to your surroundings, as shown in the middle sidebar figure. After a few seconds, the song

is recognized and displayed. You can choose to either buy the song at the Google Play Store or touch the Cancel button and start over.

The What's This Song widget works best (exclusively, I would argue) with recorded music. Try as you might, you can't sing into the thing and have it recognize a song. Humming doesn't work, either. I've tried playing the guitar and piano and — nope — those didn't work either. But for listening to ambient music, it's a good tool for discovering what you're listening to.

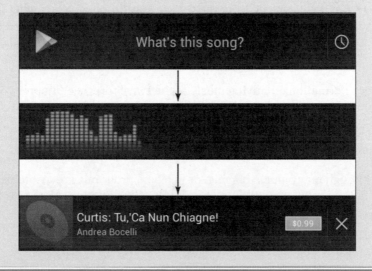

Being the life of the party

You need to do four things to make your Galaxy Tab the soul of your next shindig or soirée:

- Connect it to external speakers.
- Use the Shuffle command.
- Set the Repeat command.
- Provide plenty of drinks and snacks.

For external speakers you can use anything from a custom media dock, a stereo, or the sound system on the Times Square Jumbotron. You need an audio cable with a mini-headphone plug on one end and an audio connector for the other device on the other end. Look for such a cable at any store where the employees wear nametags.

After you connect your tablet, start the Play Music app and choose the party playlist you've created. See the later section "Organize Your Music" for information on creating playlists

Enjoy your party, and please drink responsibly.

Add Some Music to Your Life

Unless you already have music stored on Google Play, your Galaxy Tab most likely lacks tunes. Rather than just pretend you hear music, consider adding some songs and albums to the device's music library. You have two choices:

- Buy lots of music from the Google Play Store, which is what Google wants you to do
- Borrow music from your computer, which Google also wants you to do, just not as enthusiastically as the first option.

For information on buying music at the Play Store, see Chapter 15. Otherwise, you can use your computer, which is the modern-day equivalent of the old stereo system. If you've already copied your music collection to your computer, or if you use your computer as your main music storage system, you can share that music with your tablet.

Although many music-playing, or jukebox, programs are available, the most common program on Windows is Microsoft's Windows Media Player. You can use this program to synchronize music between a PC and your Tab. Here's how it works:

1. **Connect the tablet to your PC.**

   Use the USB cable that comes with the tablet.

   Over on the PC, an AutoPlay dialog box appears in Windows, prompting you to choose how best to mount the Galaxy tablet onto the Windows storage system.

2. **Close the AutoPlay dialog box.**

3. **Start Windows Media Player.**

4. **Click the Sync tab or the Sync toolbar button.**

   The Galaxy Tab appears in the Sync list on the right side of Windows Media Player, as shown in Figure 13-3.

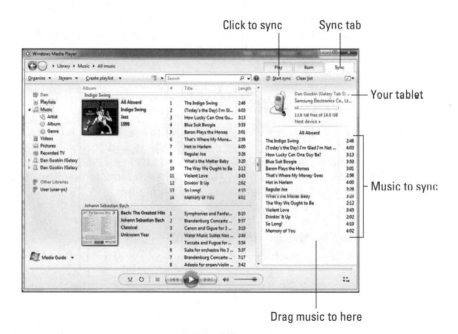

Figure 13-3: Windows Media Player meets Galaxy Tab.

5. **Drag to the Sync area the music you want to transfer to your tablet (refer to Figure 13-3).**

6. **Click the Start Sync button to transfer the music from your PC to the tablet.**

   The Sync button may be located atop the list, as shown in Figure 13-3, or it might be found on the bottom.

7. **Close Windows Media Player when you've finished transferring music.**

   Or you can keep it open — whatever.

8. **Unplug the USB cable.**

   Or you can leave the tablet plugged in.

The steps for synchronizing music with other media jukebox programs work similarly to those outlined in the preceding list.

➤ The process of connecting your tablet to a PC is covered in more detail in Chapter 17.

➤ The Galaxy Tab can store only so much music! Don't be overzealous when copying your tunes. In Windows Media Player (refer to Figure 13-3), a capacity thermometer-thing shows you how much storage space is used and how much is available on your tablet. Pay heed to the indicator!

➤ Windows Media Player complains when you try to sync the Galaxy Tab to more than one PC. If you do, you're warned after Step 6 in this section. It's not a big issue: Just inform Windows Media Player that you intend to sync with the computer for only this session.

Organize Your Music

The Play Music app categorizes your music by album, artist, song, and so forth, but unless you have only one album and enjoy all the songs on it, that configuration probably won't do. To better organize your music, you can create *playlists*. That way, you can hear the music you want to hear, in the order you want, for whatever mood hits you.

Reviewing your playlists

To view any playlists that you've already created or that have been preset on the tablet, tap the Side Menu icon and choose Playlists from the navigation drawer. You'll see the playlists displayed on the screen, as shown in Figure 13-4.

To see which songs are in a playlist, tap the playlist icon. To play the songs in the playlist, tap the first song in the list.

A playlist is a helpful way to organize music when a song's information may not have been completely imported into the tablet. For example, if you're like me, you probably have a lot of songs labeled *Unknown*. A quick way to remedy that situation is to name a playlist after the artist and then add those unknown songs to the playlist. The next section describes how it's done.

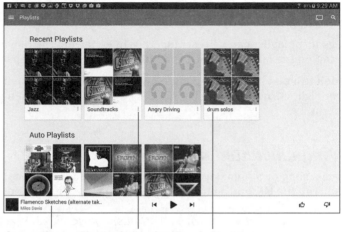

Current song　　Playlist Action Overflow　　Playlist name

Figure 13-4: Playlists in the Play Music app.

Creating your own playlists

Making a new playlist is easy, and adding songs to the playlist is even easier. Follow these steps:

1. **Find an album or song in the library.**

   Locate music you want to add to a playlist.

2. **Tap the Action Overflow icon and choose Add to Playlist.**

3. **Choose New Playlist.**

4. **Type a name for the playlist.**

5. **Type a description.**

6. **Tap the Create Playlist button.**

   The new playlist is created and the song or entire album is added to the playlist.

To add additional songs, or to build upon an existing playlist, repeat Steps 1 and 3, but in Step 3 choose an existing playlist.

- You can have as many playlists as you like on the tablet and stick as many songs as you like into them. Adding songs to a playlist doesn't noticeably affect the tablet's storage capacity.

- To remove a song from a playlist, open the playlist and tap the Action Overflow icon next to the song and choose Remove from Playlist.

- Removing a song from a playlist doesn't delete the song from the Music library.

- Songs in a playlist can be rearranged: While viewing the playlist, drag the tab on the far-left end of a song title up or down in the list.

- To delete a playlist, tap the Action Overflow icon in the playlist icon's lower-right corner (refer to Figure 13-4). Choose Delete, then tap OK to confirm.

Removing unwanted music

To remove a song or album, tap its Action Overflow icon. Choose the Delete command. Tap the OK button to remove the song. Bye-bye music.

I don't recommend removing music. Most music on your Tab is actually stored in the cloud, in Google's Play Music service. Therefore, removing the music doesn't affect the tablet's storage. So unless you despise the song or artist, removing the music has no effect.

See Chapter 15 for information on where music is stored, how to download it to the Tab, or other information.

Soap, No Soap, Galaxy Radio

Although they're not broadcast radio stations, some sources on the Internet — *Internet radio* sites — play music. Lamentably, your Galaxy Tab doesn't come with any Internet radio apps, but that doesn't stop you from finding a few good ones at the Google Play Store. Some free services that I can recommend are

- Pandora Radio
- Spotify
- TuneIn Radio

Pandora Radio and Spotify let you select music based on your mood and preferences. The more feedback you give the apps, the better the music selections.

The TuneIn Radio app gives you access to hundreds of Internet radio stations broadcasting around the world. They're organized by category, so you can find just about whatever you want. Many of the radio stations are also broadcast radio stations, so odds are good you can find a local station or two, which you can listen to on your Galaxy Tab.

These apps are available at the Google Play Store. They're free, though paid versions might also be available.

- ✔ It's best to listen to Internet radio when your tablet is connected to the Internet via a Wi-Fi connection. Streaming music can use a lot of your cellular data plan's data allotment.

- ✔ See Chapter 15 for more information about the Google Play Store.

- ✔ Internet music of the type delivered by the apps mentioned in this section is referred to by the nerds as *streaming music*. That's because the music arrives on your Galaxy tablet as a continuous download from the source. Unlike music you download and save, streaming music is played as it comes in and is not stored long-term.

14

What Else Does It Do?

Most gizmos are designed to solve a single problem. The food processor slices, grates, or chops food, but it doesn't play music (though I'm sure John Cage would argue that point). The lawn mower is good at cutting the grass but terrible at telling time. And if you have a tuba, it can play music, but it's a poor substitute for a hair dryer. That's all well and good because people accept limitations on devices designed with a specific purpose.

The Galaxy Tab is a gizmo with many purposes. Its capabilities are limited only by the apps installed. To help you grasp this concept, the tablet comes with a host of apps that can give you an idea of the tablet's capabilities. Or you can simply use those apps to make the tablet a more versatile and useful device.

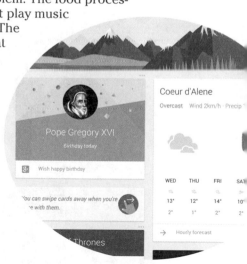

It's an Alarm Clock

Your Galaxy Tab keeps constant, accurate track of the time, which is displayed at the top of the Home screen as well as on the Lock screen. The display is lovely and informative, but it can't actually wake you up. You need to choose a specific time and apply a noise to that time. This process turns the tablet into an alarm clock.

Alarm clock duties are the responsibility of the Clock or Alarm app, depending on your Tab. You'll find the app on the Apps screen. Its main screen looks similar to what's shown in Figure 14-1. The right side of the figure shows the alarm creation and editing screen.

To create an alarm, tap the Add (+) icon, shown in Figure 14-1. Use the card that appears to edit details about the alarm. Set the schedule, sound, and other details. The most important thing to set is the date and time. Give the alarm a name. Tap the Save button to save the alarm.

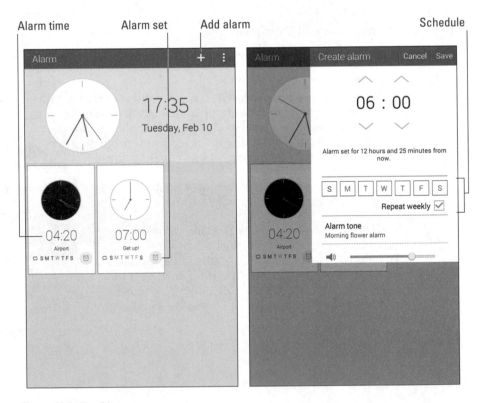

Figure 14-1: The Alarm app.

As an example, to set an alarm that wakes you up at 6:45 weekday mornings, tap the day icons, M through F (see Figure 14-1, right), and then place a check mark by Repeat Weekly. Scroll down to the bottom of the card and type a name, such as *Get Outta Bed*. Tap the Save button and the alarm is created and set.

The alarm you create appears on the app's main screen, similar to what's shown in Figure 14-1, left. Any new alarm you create is automatically set — it goes off when the proper time approaches. To disable an alarm, touch the Alarm Set icon (labeled in Figure 14-1).

Alarms must be set or they won't trigger. If you've turned off an alarm, remember to set it again; touch the Alarm Set icon, as shown in Figure 14-1.

- The app is named Clock on the Galaxy Tab S; it's named Alarm on the Galaxy Tab 4. The apps are the same.

- When an alarm is set, an Alarm status icon appears atop the screen, similar to what appears in the margin.

- Turning off an alarm doesn't delete the alarm.

- Tap an alarm to edit it.

- To remove an alarm, long-press its card and the app enters selection mode. Tap additional alarms to select them. Tap the Delete (trash can) icon to remove the alarm(s).

- The alarm doesn't work when you turn off the tablet. The alarm does work, however, when the tablet is locked. It sounds even if you've muted the tablet.

- The Location Alarm feature, found on the Create Alarm and Edit Alarm cards, can be used to disable the alarm when you're at or near certain places. Tap the Master Control icon to activate that feature, and then use the map to specify a location. As long as you're at that location, the alarm will not go off. I've had mixed results with this feature, mostly because the tablet can be iffy about knowing its exact location.

- Also see Chapter 23 for information on Blocking mode.

It's a Very Big Calculator

The Calculator is perhaps the oldest of all computer programs. Even my stupid cellphone back in the 1990s had a calculator program. (I won't dignify it by calling it an "app.")

Start the Calculator app by choosing its icon from the Apps screen. The Calculator appears, as shown in Figure 14-2. When used in a vertical orientation, the app loses the scary math buttons.

Type your equations by tapping the various buttons on the screen. The parentheses button helps set which part of a long equation gets calculated first. Use the C button to clear input.

✔ Long-press the calculator's text (or results) to cut or copy the results.

✔ I use the Calculator most often to determine my tip at a restaurant. In Figure 14-2, a calculation is being made for an 18 percent tip on an $89.56 tab.

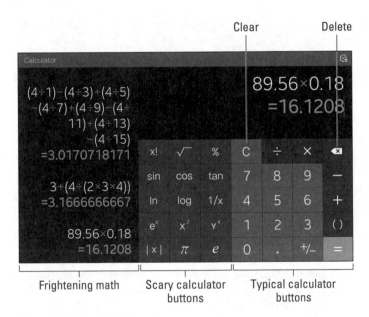

Figure 14-2: The Calculator.

It's a Calendar

Toss out your old datebook. You never need to buy another one again. That's because your Tab is the ideal datebook and appointment calendar. Thanks to the Calendar app and the Google Calendar feature on the Internet, you can manage all your scheduling right on your Galaxy tablet. It's almost cinchy.

✔ You automatically have a Google Calendar; it comes with your Google account. You can visit Google Calendar on the web at `http://calendar.google.com` but use the Calendar app instead.

✔ Before you throw away your datebook, copy into the Calendar app some future appointments and info, such as birthdays and anniversaries.

Browsing your schedule

To see what's happening next, to peruse upcoming important events, or just to know which day of the month it is, summon the Calendar app. It's located on the Apps screen along with all the other apps that dwell on your Galactic tablet.

Figure 14-3 shows the Calendar app in Month view, which gives a good overview of your schedule.

Figure 14-3: The Calendar app.

Change views by choosing a category from the top of the screen, shown in Figure 14-3. When the Tab is held in the vertical (tall) orientation, the categories appear as an action bar: Tap the action bar to choose Year, Month, Week, Day, or Agenda.

✔ Use Month view to see an overview of what's going on, and use Week or Day view to see your appointments.

✔ I check Week view at the start of the week to remind me of what's coming up.

✔ To scroll from month to month, swipe the screen up or down. In Week view and Day view, scroll from left to right.

✔ Touch the Today button to be instantly whisked back to the current day.

✔ The current date, if it's visible on the screen, appears shaded blue, as shown in Figure 14-3. In Week and Day view, a horizontal red bar marks the current time.

✔ Different colors flag your events, as seen by the bars next to event names in Figure 14-3. The colors represent a calendar category to which the events are assigned. See the later section "Creating an event" for information on calendar categories.

Reviewing appointments

To see more detail about an event, touch it. When you're using Month view, touch the event's date to see the Week view. Then choose the event again to see its details, similar to the event shown in Figure 14-4.

The details you see depend on how much information was recorded when the event was created. Some events have only a minimum of information; others may have details, such as a location for the event. When the event's location is listed, you can touch that location, and the Maps app pops up to show you where the event is being held.

Edit event

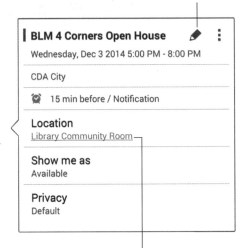

| **BLM 4 Corners Open House** ✏ ⋮
Wednesday, Dec 3 2014 5:00 PM - 8:00 PM

CDA City

⏰ 15 min before / Notification

Location
Library Community Room

Show me as
Available

Privacy
Default

Touch to see event location on the Maps app

Figure 14-4: Event details.

 Press the Back button to dismiss the event's details.

✔ Birthdays and a few other events on the calendar may be pulled from the Contacts app or even from some social networking apps. That probably explains why some events are listed twice — they're pulled in from two sources.

✔ The best way to review upcoming appointments is to choose the Agenda view.

 ✏ To quickly view upcoming events from the Home screen, slap down the
 Calendar widget. See Chapter 18 for information on applying widgets to
 the tablet's Home screen.

 ✏ Google Now also lists any immediate appointments or events. See the
 later section "It's Google Now."

Creating an event

The key to making the Calendar app work is to add events: appointments,
things to do, or meetings, or full-day events such as birthdays or colonosco-
pies. To create an event, follow these steps in the Calendar app:

1. **Select the day for the event.**

   Or if you like, you can switch to Day view, where you can touch the
   starting time for the new event.

2. **Tap the Add (+) icon.**

   The Add Event screen appears. Your job is to fill in the blanks to create
   the event.

   Don't worry if you see a message about synchronizing with Samsung
   Kies. You don't need to use Kies to use your tablet. Place a check mark
   by the item Do Not Show Again, and tap the OK button.

3. **Choose an event calendar or a calendar category.**

   Do not choose My Calendar or the Device calendar. If you do, the event
   won't be synchronized with your Google account and other devices.

4. **Type an event title.**

   Sometimes I simply write the name of the person I'm meeting.

5. **Type a location for the event.**

   My advice is to type information in the event's Location field just as
   though you're typing information to search for in the Maps app. When
   the event is displayed, the location is a link; touch the link to see where
   it is on a map.

6. **Tap Start to set the event's duration.**

   Use the controls on the card to pinpoint the starting date and time,
   although if you followed my advice in Step 1, your duties are minimal.

   When an event lasts all day, such as a birthday or your mother-in-law's
   visit that was supposed to last for an hour, tap All Day to add a check
   mark. Skip to Step 8.

7. **Tap the To button on the card to set the event's ending time.**

8. **Tap the Set button.**

   You could stop here, but if you need to set other options, such as a reminder or a repeating event, keep working through the steps.

9. **Tap the View More Options button.**

   You can set a reminder for a given duration before the event. You can set whether or not the event repeats.

10. **Touch the Done button to create the new event.**

 You can change an event at any time: Simply touch the event to bring up more information, similar to what's shown in Figure 14-4. Tap the Edit icon to modify the event.

To remove an event, tap the Action Overflow icon on its card (refer to Figure 14-4) and choose the Delete command. Touch the OK button to confirm.

 ✔ The more information you supply, the more detailed the event and the more you can do with it on your tablet as well as on Google Calendar on the Internet.

✔ It's necessary to set an event's time zone only when that event takes place in another time zone or when an event spans time zones, such as an airline flight. In that case, the Calendar app automatically adjusts the starting and stopping times for events, depending on where you are.

 ✔ If you forget to set the time zone and you end up hopping around the world, your events are set according to the time zone in which they were created, not the local time.

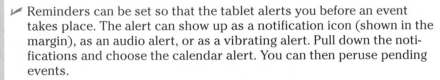 ✔ Reminders can be set so that the tablet alerts you before an event takes place. The alert can show up as a notification icon (shown in the margin), as an audio alert, or as a vibrating alert. Pull down the notifications and choose the calendar alert. You can then peruse pending events.

 ✔ Calendar categories are handy because they let you organize and color-code your events. They're confusing because Google calls them "calendars." I think of them more as categories. So I have different calendars (categories) for my personal and work schedules, government duties, clubs, and so on.

It's a Game Machine

Although you may have purchased your Galaxy Tab for business, I see nothing wrong with putting the device to work — I mean really stretching its graphical muscles — to play some games. The more advanced the mind, the more the need for play, right? So indulge yourself.

Lamentably, no sample games ship with your tablet. That may change in the future, but for now you're left to hunt down games at the Play Store just like everyone else in the Android Kingdom.

Just to be a tease, Figure 14-5 shows a game on the Galaxy tablet. It's one of many, so don't think I'm recommending anything, though I did play Jet Car Stunts on my Galaxy Tab for hours on end during a boring intercontinental flight.

✔ See Chapter 15 for information on using the Google Play Store to hunt down some exciting games. You can also use the Play Games app on the Apps screen. (The Play Games app may be in the Google folder.)

✔ Free or "lite" versions of popular games exist. Before plunking down your hard-earned 99 cents, consider testing the free version.

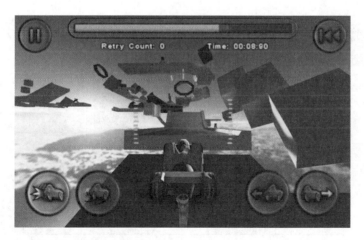

Figure 14-5: A game on a tablet.

It's an Ebook Reader

Your Galaxy Tab comes with Google's own ebook reader app, Play Books. It's found on the Apps screen, or you might find a launcher icon on the Home screen or in the Home screen's Google folder.

Begin your reading experience by opening the Play Books app. You'll see any recent books you've read. Otherwise, you can view your entire book library: Tap the Side Menu icon (shown in the margin) and choose the My Library command from the navigation drawer.

The library lists any titles you've obtained for your Google Books account, similar to what's shown in Figure 14-6.

Scroll through your library by swiping the screen.

Tap a book's cover to open it. If you've opened the book previously, you're returned to the page you last read. Otherwise, you see the book's first page.

Figure 14-7 illustrates the basic book-reading operation in the Play Books app. You turn pages by swiping the screen right to left, assuming that you're reading English or other languages that read in that direction.

The Play Books app also works in both vertical and horizontal orientations. You can lock the screen by choosing the Settings command from the navigation drawer; then choose the Auto-Rotate Screen item and select how you want the screen locked.

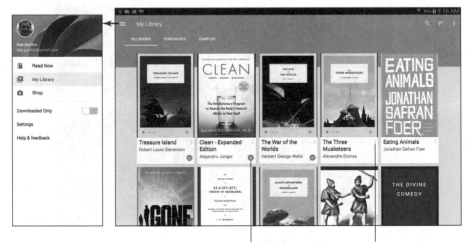

Navigation Drawer   Downloaded book Book's Action Overfow

Figure 14-6: The Play Books library.

Adjust text display

Table of contents

Search the book

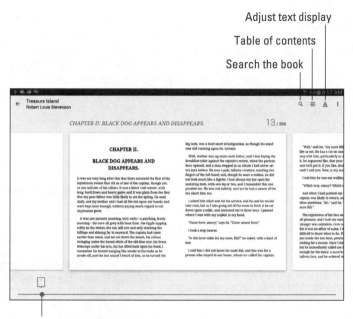

Drag to scroll through the book

Figure 14-7: Reading an ebook in the Play Books app.

✔ If you don't see a book in the library, tap the Action Overflow icon and choose Refresh.

✔ Books in your Play Books library are stored on the Internet and available to read only when an Internet connection is active. It's possible to keep a book on your Tab by downloading it to the device. Refer to Chapter 15 for details on downloading books.

✔ To remove a book from the library, touch the Action Overflow icon on the book's cover and then choose the Delete from Library command.

✔ If the onscreen controls (refer to Figure 14-7) disappear, touch the screen to see them again.

✔ Tap the <u>A</u> icon to display a menu of options for adjusting the text on the screen and the brightness.

✔ Unlike dead tree books, ebooks lack an index. That's because text on digital pages can change based on the book's presentation. Therefore, use the Search icon (refer to Figure 14-7) to look for items in the text.

✔ If you have a Kindle (and for that I must ask, "Why?" but I digress), you can obtain the Amazon Kindle app for your Tab. Use the app to access books you've purchased for the Kindle or just as a supplement to Google Books.

It's Google Now

Don't worry about your Galaxy Tab controlling too much of your life: The tablet harbors no insidious intelligence, and the Robot Uprising is still years away. Until then, you can use your tablet's listening capabilities to enjoy a feature called Google Now. It's not quite like having your own personal Jeeves, but it's on its way.

Google Now must be activated on your Galaxy Tab. To do so, start the Google app, found on the Apps screen or in the Google folder on the Home screen. Obey the prompts on the screen to obtain Google Now. You might have to tap the Get Google Now link first.

You have plenty of options for starting Google Now. The most obvious is to open the Google Now app. You can also long-press the Home button. The Google Search widget on the Home screen also acts as a doorway into Google Now.

A typical Google Now screen is shown in Figure 14-8. Below the Search text box, you'll find cards. The variety and number of cards depend on how often you use Google Now. The more you use the app, the more cards that appear.

You can use Google Now to search the Internet, just as you'd use Google's main web page. More interesting than that, you can ask Google Now questions; see the sidebar, "Barking orders to Google Now."

Search for something   Ask a question

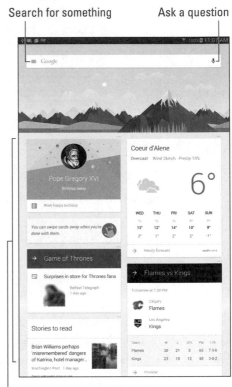

Cards

Figure 14-8: Google Now is ready for business. Or play.

✔ You can use Google Now features also by touching the Google Search widget. That widget normally comes preinstalled on the Home screen. If not, you can add it there; see Chapter 19.

✔ You cannot manually add cards to the Google Now screen. The best way to get more cards to show up is to use Google Now to search for items of interest.

Barking orders to Google Now

One way to have a lot of fun is to use the Google Now app verbally. Just say "Okay Google." Say it out loud. Any time you see the Google Now app, it's listening to you. Or when the app is being stubborn, tap the Dictation (microphone) icon.

You can speak simple search terms, such as "Find pictures of Megan Fox." Or you can give more complex orders, among them:

✔ Will it rain tomorrow?

✔ What time is it in Frankfurt, Germany?

✔ How many euros equal $25?

✔ What is 103 divided by 6?

✔ How can I get to Disneyland?

✔ Where is the nearest Canadian restaurant?

✔ What's the score of the Lakers–Celtics game?

✔ What is the answer to life, the universe, and everything?

When asked such questions, Google Now responds with a card as well as a verbal reply. When a verbal reply isn't available, Google search results are displayed.

It's Your Video Entertainment

It's not possible to watch "real" TV on your Tab, but a few apps come close. The YouTube app is handy for watching random, meaningless drivel, which I suppose makes it a lot like TV. Then there's the Play Movies & TV app, which lets you buy and rent real movies and TV shows from the Google Play Store. And when you tire of those apps, you can use the Camera app with the front-facing camera to pretend that you're the star of your own reality TV show.

Also see Chapter 23 for information on using the WatchON app, which turns your Galaxy Tab into the ultimate TV remote control.

Enjoying YouTube

YouTube is the Internet phenomenon that proves that real life is indeed too boring and random for television. Or is that the other way around? Regardless, you can view the latest videos on YouTube — or contribute your own — by using the YouTube app on your Galactic tablet.

Search for videos in the YouTube app by touching the Search icon. Type the video name, a topic, or any search terms to locate videos. Zillions of videos are available.

The YouTube app displays suggestions for any channels you're subscribed to, which allows you to follow favorite topics or YouTube content providers.

✓ Use the YouTube app to view YouTube videos, rather than use the Chrome app to visit the YouTube website.

✓ Ensure that the tablet is oriented horizontally to view the video in a larger size.

✓ Because you have a Google account, you also have a YouTube account. I recommend that you log in to your YouTube account when using the YouTube app: Touch the Menu button and choose the Sign In command. Log in if you don't see your account information.

✓ Not all YouTube videos are available for viewing on mobile devices.

Watching a flick

The Play Movies & TV app is used to watch videos you've rented or purchased at the Google Play Store. View material you've rented by opening the app and choosing the rental. Items you've purchased show up in the app's library.

Choose an item to view it on your Tab. Or you can use a screen-casting gizmo, such as Google Chromecast, to watch the video on a large screen TV or monitor.

Details for renting and purchasing movies and shows are found in Chapter 15.

At the Google Play Store

In This Chapter

▶ Shopping at the Play Store

▶ Downloading apps

▶ Buying apps, music, and books

▶ Renting movies and TV shows

▶ Building a wish list

▶ Sending an app suggestion to a friend

▶ Keeping media on your tablet

The place to find more digital stuff for your Galaxy Tab is the digital marketplace known as the Google Play Store. You can obtain music, books, movies, TV shows, and most importantly, apps. A lot of the stuff available is free. Some of it costs money but not as much as you would expect. Bottom line: The Google Play Store is the place to go when you need to expand upon your Tab's capabilities.

Welcome to the Play Store

People love to shop when they're buying something they want or when they're spending someone else's money. You can go shopping for your Galaxy Tab, and I'm not talking about going to your local Phone Store to buy overpriced accessories. I'm talking apps, games, music, magazines, movies, TV shows, and books.

The Google Play Store may sound like a place to go for buying children's outerwear, but it's really an online bazaar where you pick up new goodies for your tablet. You can browse, you can get free stuff, or you can pay. It all happens at the Play Store.

✔ Officially, it's the Google Play Store. It may also be referenced as Google Play. The app is named Play Store.

✔ The Google Play Store was once known as Android Market, and you may still see it referred to that way.

✔ You obtain items from the Google Play Store by *downloading* them to your tablet. That file transfer works best at top speeds; therefore:

✔ If you have an LTE Tab, I highly recommend that you connect it to a Wi-Fi network if you plan to obtain apps, books, or movies at the Play Store. Not only does Wi-Fi give you speed, but it also helps avoid data surcharges. See Chapter 16 for details on connecting your tablet to a Wi-Fi network.

✔ The Play Store app is frequently updated, so its look may change from what you see in this chapter. Refer to my website for updated info and tips: `www.wambooli.com/help/android/`.

Browsing the Google Play Store

You access the Google Play Store by opening the Play Store app, found on the Apps screen. A launcher icon for the Play Store might also be available on the Home screen.

After opening the Play Store app, you see the main screen, similar to the one shown in Figure 15-1. If not, tap the left arrow icon in the upper-left corner of the screen until you see the main screen. Or, if you see the Side Menu icon (shown in the margin), tap it and choose Store Home from the navigation drawer.

To browse, tap a category atop the screen. Categories available include apps, games, movies, TV shows, music, books, and magazines. Suggestions are offered below the main categories, as shown in Figure 15-1. Swipe the suggestions up and down to peruse the lot.

As an example, suppose you wanted to browse for an app: Choose the Apps category. The next screen lists popular and featured items plus additional categories you can browse by swiping the screen right to left. The category titles appear toward the top of the screen.

When you have an idea of what you want, such as an app's name or even what it does, searching works fastest: Touch the Search (magnifying glass) icon at the top of the Play Store screen (refer to Figure 15-1). Type all or part of the app's name or perhaps a description.

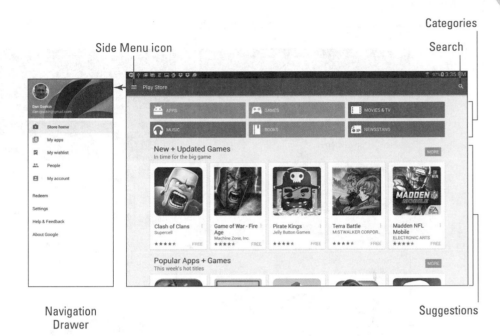

Categories

Search

Side Menu icon

Navigation
Drawer

Suggestions

Figure 15-1: The Google Play Store.

To see more information about an item, touch it. Touching something doesn't buy it but instead displays a more detailed description, screen shots, a video preview, comments, plus links to similar items, as shown in Figure 15-2.

- ✔ The first time you enter the Google Play Store, or immediately after an upgrade, you have to accept the terms of service; tap the Accept button.

- ✔ You can be assured that all apps that appear in the Google Play Store can be used with your Galaxy Tab. There's no way to download or buy something that's incompatible.

- ✔ Pay attention to an app's ratings. Ratings are added by people who use the apps — people like you and me. Having more stars is better. You can see additional information, including individual user reviews, by selecting the app.

- ✔ Another good indicator of an app's success is how many times it's been downloaded. Some apps have been downloaded over ten million times. That's a good sign.

- ✔ In Figure 15-2, the app's description (on the right) shows the Install button. Other buttons that may appear on an app's description screen include Open, Update, and Uninstall. The Open button opens an app that's already installed on your tablet; the Update button updates an already installed app; and the Uninstall button removes an installed app. See Chapter 18 for more information on app management.

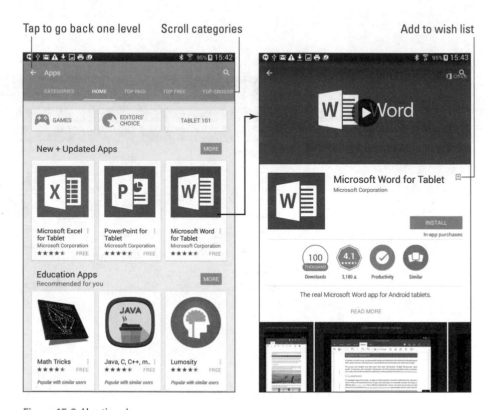

Figure 15-2: Hunting down an app.

Obtaining an app

After you locate an app you want, the next step is to download it, by copying it from the Google Play Store on the Internet to your Galactic tablet. The app is installed automatically, building up your collection of apps and expanding what the tablet can do.

Good news: Most apps are available for free. Better news: Even the apps you pay for don't cost dearly. In fact, it seems odd to sit and stew over whether paying 99 cents for a game is worth it.

I recommend that you download a free app first, to familiarize yourself with the process. Then try your hand at a paid app.

Free or not, the process of obtaining an app works pretty much the same. Follow these steps:

1. **Open the Play Store app.**

2. **Find the app you want and open its description.**

   The app's description screen looks similar to the one shown on the right side in Figure 15-2.

   The difference between a free app and a paid app is found on the button used to obtain the app. For a free app, the button says Install. For a paid app, the button shows the price.

3. **Tap the Install button to get a free app; for a paid app, touch the button with the price on it.**

   Don't fret! You're not buying anything yet.

   You see a screen describing the app's permissions. The list isn't a warning, and it doesn't mean anything bad. The Play Store is just informing you which of your tablet's features the app will have access to.

4. **Tap the Accept button.**

   If you're purchasing an app, you must tap the Buy button to complete the purchase. See the next section for details.

5. **Wait while the app downloads.**

   The Downloading notification appears atop the screen as the app is downloaded. You're free to do other things on your Galaxy Tab while the app is downloaded and installed.

6. **Touch the Open button to run the app.**

   Or if you were doing something else while the app was downloading and installing, choose the Successfully Installed notification, as shown in the margin. The notification features the app's name with the text *Successfully Installed* below it.

At this point, what happens next depends on the app you've downloaded. For example, you may have to agree to a license agreement. If so, touch the I Agree button. Additional setup may involve setting your location, signing in to an account, or creating a profile, for example.

After you complete the initial app setup, or if no setup is necessary, you can start using the app.

- All apps you obtain from the Play Store can be found on the Apps screen.

- Your Tab most likely installed an app launcher icon on the Home screen. Refer to Chapter 18 for information on removing or moving the launcher icon.

- Also see Chapter 18 for information on uninstalling apps.

Purchasing something at the Play Store

When you purchase something at the Play Store, such as an app, music, or an ebook, you tap a Buy button. A card appears listing available payment methods. These include any credit cards you've used in the past, plus Google credit you may have redeemed earlier.

Figure 15-3 shows the Buy card for purchasing an app. The app costs $2.27. The chosen payment method is Google Play Balance, which is cash left over from a gift card. That payment method is used automatically once the Buy button is tapped.

To select another payment method, follow these steps when the Buy card is presented:

1. **Tap the chevron by the price.**

   The chevron is shown at the top of Figure 15-3.

2. **Choose Payment Methods.**

   Of, if you're fortunate enough to have a Google Play gift card, tap Redeem to cash in.

3. **Choose a credit or debit card, PayPal, or a gift card.**

   The credit or debit cards listed are those you've used before. Don't worry: Your stuff is safe.

   If you don't yet have a credit or debit card registered, choose the option Add Credit or Debit Card, and complete the onscreen steps to set up your payment.

Current payment method

Choose another form of payment

Figure 15-3: The Play Store's Buy card.

Never buy anything twice

Any apps, music, books, or other items you buy from the Play Store are yours as long as you keep your Google account or until the Robot Uprising, whichever comes first. That means that you don't have to buy anything a second time.

For example, if you have an Android phone and you already paid for a slew of apps, you can obtain those same apps for your Galaxy Tab: Just visit the Play Store and install the apps.

The same rule goes for music, books, or anything you've previously paid for.

To review already purchased apps in the Play Store, choose the My Apps item in the sidebar (refer to Figure 15-1, left). Tap the All tab at the top of the screen. You'll see all the apps you've ever obtained at the Google Play Store, including apps you've previously paid for. Those apps are flagged with the text *Purchased.* Select the item to reinstall the paid app.

4. **Type your Google password.**

   This step provides for security. I strongly recommend that you never choose the option Never Ask Me Again.

5. **If prompted, tap the Every Time option.**

   By choosing this option, you ensure that your password is required for every purchase you make at the Play Store.

At this, point, the item you purchased is made available. Apps are instantly downloaded and installed; music, ebooks, movies, and videos are available but not necessarily downloaded. See the later section, "Keeping stuff on the device."

🖝 Eventually, you'll receive a Gmail message from the Google Play Store, confirming your purchase. The message contains a link you can select to review the refund policy in case you change your mind about the purchase.

🖝 Be quick on that refund: For a purchased app, you have only two hours to get your money back. You know when the time limit is up because the Refund button on the app's description screen changes to Uninstall.

Getting music for your Tab

The Play Store is also the go-to app for obtaining music for Tab. To search for music, follow these steps:

1. **Tap the Music category on the main Play Store screen.**

   You can also view the Play Store's music category from the Play Music app: Tap the Side Menu icon, shown in the margin, and choose Shop from the navigation drawer.

2. Use the Search icon to help you locate music, or just browse the categories.

Eventually you'll see a page showing details about the song or album, similar to what's shown in Figure 15-4.

Choose a song from the list to hear a preview. The button next to the song or album indicates the purchase price, or it says Free for free music.

3. Touch the Free button to get a free song, or touch the price button to purchase a song or an album.

Don't worry; you're not buying anything yet.

4. To buy music, choose your credit card or payment source.

Refer to the preceding section, "Obtaining an app," for purchase details.

5. Touch the Buy or Confirm button.

The song or album is added to your Tab's music library.

Refer to Chapter 13 for more information on using your Galaxy Tab as a portable music player.

Buy the whole album

Add to wish list

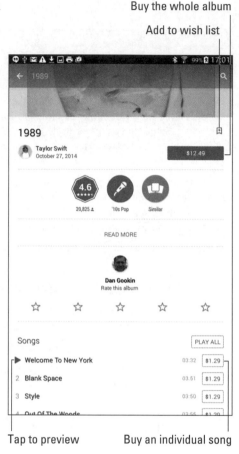

Tap to preview   Buy an individual song

Figure 15-4: Music in the Play Store.

- You'll eventually receive a Gmail message listing a summary of your purchase.

- All music sales are final. Don't blame me; I'm just writing down Google's current policy for music purchases.

- Keep an eye out for special offers at the Play Store. They're a great way to pick up some free tunes.

- Music you purchase from the Google Play Music store is available on any Android device with the Play Music app installed, providing you use the same Google account on that device. You can also listen to your tunes by visiting the music.google.com site on any computer connected to the Internet.

Buying books and renting videos

The process for buying books works the same as that for buying an app or music: Search for a title or browse the Books section of the Play Store app. Some books, particularly classics, are available free. Others must be purchased; refer to the earlier section "Purchasing something at the Play Store" for details.

When it comes to movies and TV shows, you have two options: rent or purchase.

When you choose to rent a video, the rental is available to view for the next 30 days. Once you start watching, however, you have only 24 hours to finish — you can also watch the video over and over again during that time span.

Purchasing a video is more expensive than renting it, but you can view the movie or TV show at any time, on any Android device. You can also download the movie so that you can watch it even when an Internet connection isn't available.

One choice you must make when buying a movie is whether to purchase the SD or HD version. The SD version is cheaper, and the HD version plays at high definition only on certain output devices. The Galaxy Tab isn't one of those devices.

Play Store Tricks

You may have no desire to be a Play Store expert. Just get the app you want, grouse over having to pay 99 cents for that must-have game or $4.99 to rent the latest blockbuster, and get on with your life. When you're ready to get more from the Play Store, peruse some of the items in this section.

Using the wish list

While you dither over getting a paid app, music, book, or any other purchase at the Play Store, consider adding it to your wish list: Touch the Wish List icon when viewing the app (the Wish List icon is shown in the margin).

To review your wish list, tap the Side Menu icon in the Play Store app (refer to Figure 15-1). Choose the My Wishlist item from navigation drawer. You'll see all the items you've flagged. When you're ready to buy, choose one and buy it!

Sharing an item from the Play Store

Sometimes you love your Play Store purchase so much that you just can't contain your glee. When that happens, consider sharing the item. Obey these steps:

1. **Open the Play Store app.**

2. **Browse or search for the app, music, book, or other item you want to share.**

3. **When you find the item, tap it to view its description screen.**

 4. **Touch the Share icon.**

   You may have to swipe down the screen to locate the Share icon, shown in the margin. After tapping the Share icon, you see a menu listing various apps.

5. **Choose an app.**

   For example, choose Gmail to send a Play Store link in an email message.

6. **Use the chosen app to send the link.**

   What happens next depends on which sharing method you've chosen.

The end result of these steps is that your friend receives a link. That person can touch the link on his mobile Android device and be whisked instantly to the Google Play Store, where the item can be obtained.

Methods for using the various items on the Share menu are found throughout this book.

Keeping stuff on the device

Books, music, movies and TV shows you obtain from the Play Store are not copied to your Galaxy Tab. Instead, they're stored on the Internet. When you access the media, it's streamed into your tablet as needed. This setup works well, and it keeps your Tab from running out of storage space, but it works only when an Internet connection is available.

When you plan on being away from an Internet connection, such as when you are flying across country and are too cheap to pay for inflight Wi-Fi, you can download Play Store purchases and save them on your tablet.

To see which media is on your Tab and which isn't, open the Play Books, Play Music, or Play Movies & TV app. Follow these steps, which work the same in each app:

1. **Tap the Side Menu icon.**

2. **In the navigation drawer, slide the Master Control by Downloaded Only to the on position.**

   Just tap the gizmo and it toggles between on and off settings.

3. **Choose the My Library item from the navigation drawer.**

   You see only those items on your tablet. The rest of your library, you can assume, is located on the Internet.

Repeat these steps to reset the Downloaded Only option to off, so that you can see all your books, music, and videos.

 Items downloaded to your tablet feature an On Device icon, similar to the one shown in the margin. The icon's color changes, depending on which app you're using.

 To keep an item on your tablet, look for the Download icon, shown in the margin. Tap that icon and the item is fetched from the Internet and stored on your device.

 Keeping movies and lots of music on your Galaxy Tab consumes a lot of storage space. That's okay for short trips and such, but for the long term, consider purging some of your downloaded media.

To remove an item you've downloaded, tap the On Device icon. Tap the Remove button to confirm.

Don't worry about removing downloaded media. You can always download it again at no charge.

Part IV
Nuts and Bolts

Files on the computer

Files on the Tab

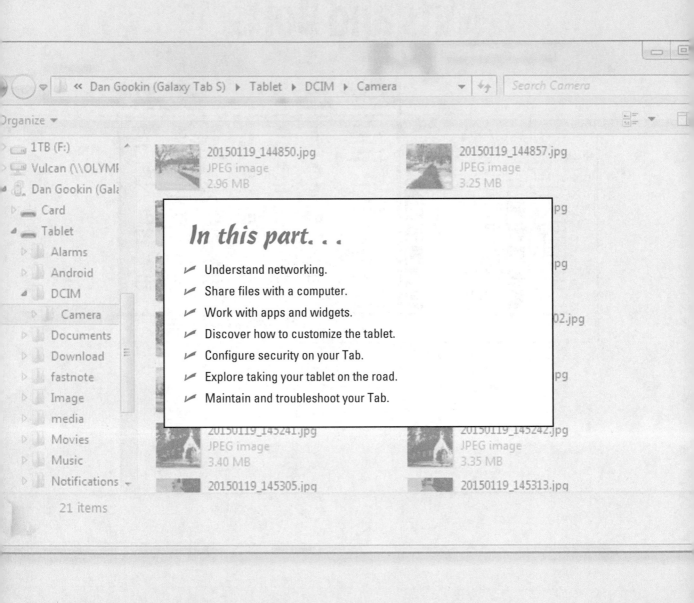

In this part. . .

- 🖊 Understand networking.
- 🖊 Share files with a computer.
- 🖊 Work with apps and widgets.
- 🖊 Discover how to customize the tablet.
- 🖊 Configure security on your Tab.
- 🖊 Explore taking your tablet on the road.
- 🖊 Maintain and troubleshoot your Tab.

16

It's a Wireless Life

In This Chapter

▶ Using the cellular data network

▶ Enabling Wi-Fi

▶ Connecting to a Wi-Fi network

▶ Accessing hidden networks

▶ Using Bluetooth

▶ Pairing a Bluetooth device

*W*hat exactly is *portable?* Back in the olden days, the boys in Marketing would say that bolting a handle to just about anything made it portable. Even a rhinoceros would be portable if he had a handle. Well, and the legs, they kind of make the rhino portable, I suppose. But my point is that to be portable requires more than just a handle; it requires a complete lack of wires.

Your Samsung Galaxy Tab's battery allows it to wander away from a wall socket. The digital cellular signal offers Internet access pretty much all over. Other types of wireless communications are available, including Wi-Fi and Bluetooth. These features ensure portability.

Wireless Networking Wizardry

You know that wireless networking has hit the big-time when you see people asking Santa Claus for a Wi-Fi router at Christmas. Such a thing would have been unheard of years ago because back then routers were used primarily for woodworking. Today, wireless networking is what keeps a gizmo such as your Galaxy Tab connected to the Internet.

Using the mobile data network

The LTE Tab is designed to connect to the Internet by using the mobile data network, the same network type used by smartphones. Several types of digital cellular networks are available:

- ✔ **4G LTE:** The fourth generation of wide-area data network and the fastest.

- ✔ **3G:** The third generation network, which is the fastest network when a 4G signal isn't available.

- ✔ **1X:** Several types of the original, slower cellular data signals are still available. They all fall under the 1X banner. It's slow.

Your tablet always uses the best network available. So, if the 4G LTE network is within reach, that network is used for Internet access. Otherwise, the 3G network is chosen, and then 1X in an act of last-ditch desperation.

- ✔ A notification icon for the type of network being used appears in the status area, right next to the Signal Strength icon.

- ✔ Accessing the digital cellular network isn't free. Your tablet most likely has some form of subscription plan for a certain quantity of data. When you exceed that quantity, the costs can become prohibitive.

- ✔ See Chapter 21 for information on how to avoid cellular data overcharges when taking your Galaxy Tab out and about.

- ✔ Also see Chapter 23 for information on monitoring your mobile data usage.

Understanding Wi-Fi

The digital cellular connection is nice, and it's available pretty much all over, but it costs you moolah. A better option, and one you should seek out when it's available, is *Wi-Fi,* or the same wireless networking standard used by computers for communicating with each other and the Internet.

Making Wi-Fi work on your Galactic tablet requires two steps. First, you must activate the tablet's Wi-Fi radio. Second, you connect the tablet to a specific wireless network. The next two sections cover both of these steps.

Wi-Fi stands for *wireless fidelity.* It's brought to you by the numbers 802.11 and various letters of the alphabet.

Activating and deactivating Wi-Fi

Follow these carefully written directions to activate Wi-Fi networking on your Galaxy Tab:

1. **Open the Settings app.**

2. **Tap the Connections tab.**

3. **Ensure that the Master Control by the Wi-Fi setting is on.**

   Green is on.

To turn off Wi-Fi, repeat these steps but set the Master Control to the off position. Turning off Wi-Fi disconnects the tablet from any wireless networks.

And now, the shortcut: Pull down the notifications shade and use the Wi-Fi Quick Setting to turn Wi-Fi on or off. When the button is green, Wi-Fi is on.

- ✔ When activated, the Tab connects automatically to any memorized Wi-Fi networks. So when you saunter back to the same café, the connection is made automatically.

- ✔ Using Wi-Fi to connect to the Internet doesn't incur data usage charges.

Connecting to a Wi-Fi network

After you've activated the tablet's Wi-Fi radio, you can connect to an available wireless network. Heed these steps:

1. **Open the Settings app.**

2. **Tap the Connections tab and choose Wi-Fi.**

   The Wi-Fi radio must be on for you to find a network. If the Master Control isn't green, touch it.

3. **Choose a wireless network from the list.**

   Available Wi-Fi networks appear on the right side of the screen, as shown in Figure 16-1. (As shown in the figure, I chose the Imperial Wambooli network, which is my office network.) When no wireless networks are listed, you're sort of out of luck regarding wireless access from your current location.

4. **If the network requires a password, type it.**

   Touch the Password text box to see the onscreen keyboard.

   Touch the Show Password check box so that you can see what you're typing; some of those network passwords can be *long*.

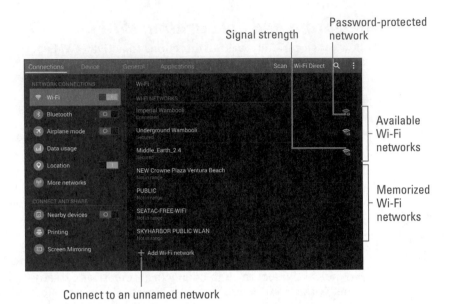

Figure 16-1: Finding a wireless network.

5. **Tap the Connect button.**

   The Tab is immediately connected to the network. If not, try the password again.

 When the tablet is connected to a wireless network, you see the Wi-Fi status icon, as shown in the margin. This icon means that the tablet's Wi-Fi is on, connected, and communicating with a Wi-Fi network.

✔ Some public networks are open to anyone, but you have to use the web browser app to access a login page before you're granted full access: Open the web browser app, browse to any page on the Internet, and the login page shows up.

✔ Your tablet automatically remembers every Wi-Fi network it has ever been connected to and automatically reconnects upon finding the same network again.

 ✔ Not every wireless network has a password. They should! Generally speaking, I don't avoid connecting to any public network that lacks a password, but I don't use that network for shopping, banking, or any other online activity that should be conducted securely.

✔ To disconnect from a Wi-Fi network, simply turn off Wi-Fi. See the preceding section.

> ✔ Unlike a cellular data network, a Wi-Fi network's broadcast signal goes only so far. My advice is to use Wi-Fi whenever you plan to remain in one location for a while. If you wander too far, your tablet loses the signal and is disconnected.

Connecting to a hidden Wi-Fi network

Some wireless networks don't broadcast their names, which adds security but also makes connecting more difficult. In these cases, select the Add Wi-Fi Network option (refer to Figure 16-1) to manually add the network. Type the network name, or *SSID,* and choose the type of security. You also need the password if one is used. You can obtain this information from the person in charge of the wireless network at your location, such as girl with the pink hair who sold you coffee.

Connecting to a WPS router

Many Wi-Fi routers feature WPS, which stands for Wi-Fi Protected Setup. It's a network authorization system that's really simple and quite secure. If the wireless router uses WPS, and you can find the WPS icon as shown in the margin, you can use this feature it to quickly connect your Tab to the network.

To make a WPS connection, obey these steps:

1. **Open the Settings app and tap the Connections tab.**
2. **Choose Wi-Fi.**
3. **Tap the Action Overflow icon (shown in the margin).**
4. **Choose WPS Push Button.**
5. **Press the WPS button on the router.**

If the WPS router requires a PIN (personal identification number), choose WPS PIN Enter in Step 4. On the router, type the number on your Tab's screen to complete the connection.

The Bluetooth Experience

Computer nerds have long had the desire to connect high-tech gizmos to one another. The Bluetooth standard was developed to sate this desire in a wireless way. Although Bluetooth is wireless *communication,* it's not the same as wireless networking. It's more about connecting peripheral devices, such as keyboards, mice, printers, headphones, and other gear. It all happens in a wireless way, and it really has nothing to do with the color blue or anything dental.

Understanding Bluetooth

To make Bluetooth work, you need a Bluetooth peripheral, such as a wireless keyboard. The idea is to pair that peripheral with your tablet. The operation works like this:

1. **Turn on the Bluetooth wireless radio for both your tablet and the peripheral.**

2. **Make the peripheral discoverable.**

   The gizmo is saying, "Hey! I'm over here!" Well, it's saying so electronically.

3. **On your tablet, choose the peripheral from the list of Bluetooth devices.**

4. **If necessary, confirm the connection.**

   For example, you may be asked to input a code or press a button on the peripheral.

5. **Use the Bluetooth peripheral.**

You can use the Bluetooth peripheral as much as you like. Turn off the tablet. Turn off the peripheral. When you turn both on again, they're automatically reconnected.

 Bluetooth devices are usually marked with the Bluetooth logo, shown in the margin. It's your assurance that the gizmo can work with other Bluetooth devices.

Activating Bluetooth on the Tab

To make the Bluetooth connection, first turn on the Tab's Bluetooth radio. Obey these directions:

1. **Open the Settings app and tap the Connections tab.**

2. **Slide the Master Control by the Bluetooth item to the on position.**

   When the Master Control is green, Bluetooth is activated.

 When Bluetooth is on, the Bluetooth status icon appears, as shown in the margin.

To turn off Bluetooth, repeat the steps in this section: Slide the Master Control to the off position.

 From the And-Now-He-Tells-Us Department, you can quickly activate Bluetooth by using the Quick Settings on the notifications shade. Tap the Bluetooth icon to turn Bluetooth on or off.

Pairing with a Bluetooth device

To make the Bluetooth connection between your Galaxy tablet and some other gizmo, follow these steps:

1. **Ensure that Bluetooth is on.**

   Refer to the preceding section.

2. **Turn on the Bluetooth gizmo or ensure that its Bluetooth radio is on.**

   Some Bluetooth devices have separate power and Bluetooth switches.

3. **On your tablet, open the Settings app and then tap the Connections tab.**

4. **Choose Bluetooth.**

   Touch the Bluetooth item, not the green button. You'll see a list of available and paired devices shown on the right side of the screen, similar to Figure 16-2. Don't fret if the device you want doesn't yet appear in the list.

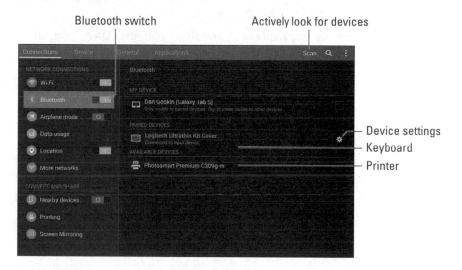

Figure 16-2: Finding Bluetooth gizmos.

5. **If the other device has an option to become visible, select it.**

   For example, some Bluetooth gizmos have a tiny button to press that makes the device visible to other Bluetooth gizmos. (You don't need to make the Galaxy Tab visible for this operation.)

6. **Select the device.**

   If the device doesn't show up, tap the Scan button.

7. If necessary, type the device's passcode or otherwise acknowledge the connection.

For example, with a Bluetooth keyboard, the Tab may prompt you to type a series of numbers on the keyboard and then press the Enter or Return key. That action completes the pairing.

When the device is paired, you can begin using it.

Connected devices appear in the Bluetooth Settings window, such as the Logitech keyboard cover shown in Figure 16-2.

✔ How you use the device depends on what it does. For example, a Bluetooth keyboard can be used for text input. You can use a Bluetooth speaker to listen to music played on the Tab.

✔ It's rare to unpair a device. Should you need to, visit the Bluetooth screen (refer to Figure 16-2) and tap the Settings icon by the device's entry. Choose the Unpair command to break the Bluetooth connection and stop using the device.

✔ Only unpair devices you don't plan on using again. Otherwise, simply turn off the Bluetooth device when you've finished using it.

✔ The Tab's Bluetooth radio consumes a lot of power. Don't forget to turn off the device, especially a battery-powered one, when you're no longer using it with your tablet.

Connect, Share, and Store

espite the Tab's wireless and mobile nature, you may desire to share information stored on your Galaxy Tab with other devices. Likewise, you might want to access from your tablet information stored elsewhere. Several methods are available to accomplish these tasks, although osmosis doesn't seem to be as effective as others. The most successful ways to connect and share are covered in this chapter, along with information on Galactic tablet storage.

The USB Connection

The most direct way to connect a Samsung Galaxy Tab to a computer is by using a wire — specifically, the wire nestled cozily in the heart of a USB cable.

Connecting the tablet to a computer

The USB connection between the Galaxy Tab and a computer works fastest when both devices are physically connected. That connection requires using the USB cable that comes with the tablet. Unlike the mythical Mobius cable, the Galaxy Tab's USB cable has two ends:

   ✔ One end of the USB cable plugs into the computer.

   ✔ The other end of the cable plugs into the bottom of the tablet.

The connectors are shaped differently and cannot be plugged in backward or upside down.

What happens after you connect your tablet to a computer is the topic of the next several sections.

✔ By connecting the tablet to a computer, you are adding, or *mounting,* its storage to the computer's storage system. The files and folders on the tablet can be accessed by using the computer's file-management commands, which is how file transfer takes place.

✔ Even if you don't use the USB cable to communicate with the computer, the tablet's battery charges when it's connected to a computer's USB port — as long as the computer is turned on, of course.

Configuring the USB connection

A computer recognizes the Galaxy Tab's USB connection in one of two ways: MTP or PTP. Between the two, the MTP method is better for transferring files. To ensure that your Tab is configured for that type of connection, follow these directions:

1. **Connect the tablet to a computer.**

2. **Choose the USB notification.**

   The USB notification icon is shown in the margin.

3. **Ensure that Media Device (MTP) is selected.**

   If not, choose that option.

Following these steps may fix the problem of a computer not recognizing the tablet.

✔ The USB notification appears when the tablet is connected to a computer.

✔ A Macintosh may recognize your Galaxy Tab only when it's configured with the Media Device USB setting.

✔ MTP stands for *Media Transfer Protocol.* When this option is set, the computer sees the tablet's storage as if it were a media card or a thumb drive.

✔ PTP stands for *Picture Transfer Protocol.* When this option is chosen, the computer believes the tablet to be a digital camera and it treats storage as if it held film and videos. I've rarely seen an instance when this setting is necessary.

Dealing with the USB connection in Windows

Upon making the USB connection between the Galaxy Tab and a PC, a number of things happen. Don't let any of these things cause you undue alarm.

First, you may see some activity on the PC: drivers being installed and such. That's normal behavior any time you first connect a new USB gizmo to a Windows computer.

Second, you may see one of two AutoPlay dialog boxes, as shown in Figure 17-1, depending on how the tablet's USB connection is configured. Both dialog boxes are similar.

Finally, choose an option from the AutoPlay dialog box or just close the dialog box. From that point on, you'll use Windows or a program on your computer to work with the files on your tablet. Later sections in this chapter provide the details.

✔ In Windows 8, things work differently: Look for a prompt on the screen that says Tap to Choose What Happens with This Device. Click or touch the prompt to view suggestions similar to those found in the AutoPlay dialog boxes (refer to Figure 17-1).

✔ Even if the AutoPlay dialog box doesn't appear, you can still access media and files stored on the tablet from your computer. The later section "Files from Here, Files to There" has details.

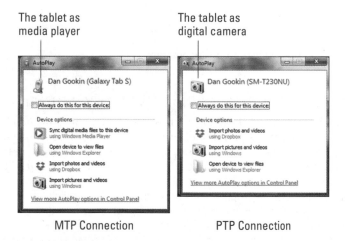

Figure 17-1: Windows AutoPlay dialog boxes.

Connecting your tablet to a Mac

Curiously enough, the Macintosh refuses to recognize the USB–Galaxy Tab connection. I wonder why?

To do the file transfer thing between your Mac and Galaxy tablet, you need to obtain the Android File Transfer app. Download that software from this website: www.android.com/filetransfer.

Install the software. Run it. From that point on, when you connect your Galactic tablet to the Macintosh, you see a special window, similar to what's shown in Figure 17-2. It lists the tablet's folders and files. Use that window for file management, as covered later in this chapter.

Internal
storage   MicroSD card storage

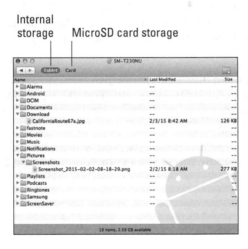

Figure 17-2: The Android File Transfer program.

Disconnecting the tablet from a computer

The process of disconnecting your tablet from a computer is cinchy: When you've finished transferring files, music, or other media, close all the programs and folders you've opened, specifically those you've used to work with the tablet's storage. Then you can disconnect the USB cable. That's it.

It's a Bad Idea to unplug the tablet while you're transferring information or while a folder window is open on a PC. Doing so could damage the tablet's internal storage, rendering some of the information kept there unreadable. So just to be safe, before disconnecting, close those programs and folder windows you've opened.

Unlike other external storage on the Macintosh, there's no need to eject the tablet's storage when you've finished accessing it. Quit the Android File Transfer program on the Mac, and then unplug the tablet — or vice versa. The Mac won't get angry.

Files from Here, Files to There

The point of making the USB connection between your Galaxy Tab and a computer is to exchange files. You can't just wish the files over. Instead, I recommend following the advice in this section.

A good understanding of basic file operations is necessary before you attempt file transfers between your computer and the Galaxy tablet. You need to know how to copy, move, rename, and delete files. It also helps to be familiar with what folders are and how they work. The good news is that you don't need to manually calculate a 64-bit cyclical redundancy check on the data, nor do you need to know what a parity bit is.

Transferring files by using the USB connection

I can think of plenty of reasons why you would want to copy a file from your computer to the tablet. You can transfer pictures and videos, music or audio files, or copy vCards exported from the computer's email program, which helps build your tablet's address book.

Follow these steps to copy files between a computer and the tablet:

1. **Connect the Galaxy Tab to the computer by using the USB cable.**

   Specific directions are offered earlier in this chapter.

2. **On a PC, if the AutoPlay dialog box appears, select the Open Folder/ Device to View Files option.**

   When the AutoPlay dialog box doesn't appear, open the Computer window, and then open the Galaxy Tabs icon. Open the Tablet or Card icon, which represents internal and external storage, respectively.

   The tablet's folder window you see looks like any other folder in Windows. The difference is that the files and folders in that window are on the Galaxy Tab, not on the computer.

   On a Macintosh, the Android File Transfer program should start and appear on the screen (refer to Figure 17-2).

3. **On the PC, open the folder that contains files you want to copy to the tablet, or into which you can to copy files from the tablet.**

   Open the folder that contains the files, or somehow have the file icons visible on the screen.

4. **Drag file icons between the two folders.**

Figure 17-3 illustrates two folder windows that are open on a PC, one on the Galaxy Tab and the other on the PC. Use the mouse to drag icons between the two folders.

The same file-dragging technique can be used for transferring files from a Macintosh. Drag the icons to or from the Android File Transfer window, which works just like any folder window in the Finder.

5. **Close the folder windows and disconnect the USB cable when you're done.**

Refer to specific instructions earlier in this chapter.

Galaxy Tab storage

Files on the computer

Files on the Tab

Figure 17-3: Copying files to a Galaxy tablet.

If you don't know where to copy files to your Tab, then I offer these recommendations:

- ✔ Copy music or audio files to the Music folder. Even then, a better way to copy music is to use a jukebox program on your computer to make the transfer. Refer to Chapter 13 for details.

- ✔ Copy images to the Pictures folder. As with music, a better option would be to use a photo management program to transfer images to the tablet in an organized fashion. Windows Media Player handles this task on a PC.

- ✔ Copy all other files to the tablet's Download folder. After all, you are technically downloading files from the computer, so that seems like an obvious choice.

The media card transfer

Another way to get files between a computer and your Galactic tablet is to use the microSD card. It can be removed from the tablet and then inserted into a computer. From that point, the files on the card can be read by the computer just as they can be read from any media card.

See Chapter 1 for details on how to remove the microSD card from your tablet. You can't just yank out the thing!

You also need a microSD adapter to insert the card into a media reader on the computer. Or you can get a microSD card thumb drive adapter, in which case you merely need a USB port to access the card's information.

Sharing files with Dropbox

A wireless way to share files between a computer and your Galaxy Tab is to use the Dropbox app. That app grants your tablet access to Internet file storage, also known as *cloud* storage. Any other device that uses that storage also has access to the files. That makes Dropbox an ideal way to share and swap files.

Your tablet comes with the Dropbox app. Open it! If you already have a Dropbox account, sign in. If not, sign up.

On your computer, obtain a copy of Dropbox by visiting the Dropbox website at www.dropbox.com. Download the program. Dropbox is free and comes with a generous amount of online storage at no charge.

The files and folders accessed by your Dropbox account are available to both your computer and tablet. Copy, move, or create a file in one of the folders, and all your Dropbox devices have access — provided an Internet connection is available.

As an example, to share a photo between your PC and tablet, copy the image to the Dropbox\photos folder. On your Tab, open the Dropbox app and tap the Photos folder. Tap your photo from the list to view it. That's how cloud storage works, and it's nearly instantaneous.

- ✔ File management on your Galaxy tablet is handled by the My Files app, in case you're into that sort of thing. See the later section, "Managing files."

- ✔ You can configure the tablet so that pictures and videos you take are instantly uploaded to Dropbox. See Chapter 12.

- ✔ Another cloud storage option is Google Drive. Because you have a Google account, you already have access to that storage. Use the Drive app on your Tab to view the storage. As with Dropbox, you can obtain Google Drive for your PC or Mac to share and swap files.

Sharing the screen

It's possible to view information displayed on your Galaxy Tab S on an HDMI TV or monitor. The Samsung-preferred way is to use the Screen Mirroring command, but it works only with the Samsung AllShare Cast gizmo. As an alternative, I suggest getting the Google Chromecast gizmo. It's geared to work well with Android apps such as Play Movies & TV,

Netflix, and Hulu Plus. It also works with the Galaxy Tab 4.

When a casting device is connected to an HDMI TV or monitor, start an app on your Tab. Tap the casting icon, shown nearby. Choose the casting device from the list, and the information shown on the tablet's screen appears on the TV or monitor.

Screen Mirroring

Chromecast

Printing

You may not think of it as "file sharing," but using a printer with your Galaxy Tab is another way to get a file from here to there. It just happens that "there" is a printer, not a computer.

Printing on your Galaxy Tab works like this:

1. **View the material you want to print.**

   You can print a web page, photo, map, or any number of items.

2. **Tap the Action Overflow icon and choose the Print action.**

3. **Choose a printer from the Select Printer list or the action bar.**

   Any printer available on the Wi-Fi network that the Tab is using shows up in the list.

   To view printers from the action bar, tap the bar, as shown in Figure 17-4. Not every Tab uses the method shown in the figure.

4. **Change any print settings.**

   For example, tap the Pages item to set the pages you want to print. Or change the number of copies. These are common print settings, similar to those you'd find in a computer's Print dialog box.

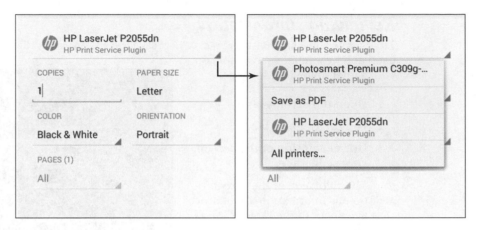

Figure 17-4: Choosing a printer.

5. Tap the Print button.

The material you're viewing prints.

Not every app supports printing. The only way to know is to work through Steps 1 and 2. If you don't see the Print action, you can't print.

Galactic Storage

Somewhere, deep in your Galaxy Tab's bosom, lies a storage device. It's like the hard drive in a computer. The thing can't be removed, but that's not the point. The point is that the storage is used for your apps, music, videos, pictures, and a host of other information. This section describes what you can do to manage that storage.

- ✔ The Galaxy Tab comes with either 16GB or 32GB of internal storage.

- ✔ Removable storage is also available in the form of a microSD card.

- ✔ A GB is a gigabyte, or one billion bytes (characters) of storage. A typical 2-hour movie occupies about 4GB of storage, but most things you store on the tablet — music and pictures, for example — take up only a sliver of storage. Those slivers can and do add up over time.

Reviewing storage stats

To discover how storage space is used and how much is available on your tablet, follow these steps:

1. **Open the Settings app.**

2. **Tap the General tab.**

3. **On the left side of the screen, choose Storage.**

   The right side of the screen details information about storage space in the tablet's internal storage, shown as Device Memory in Figure 17-5.

You can choose a category to see more information or to launch a program. For example, touch Used Space (refer to Figure 17-5) to display a list of items occupying that chunk of memory. You can choose a subcategory, such as Applications, Pictures, or Videos, to see more details.

When a microSD card is installed, information about its storage appears in the SD Card area, barely visible in the bottom right in Figure 17-5. Alas, further detail is unavailable. You'll have to use the My Files app to review the storage device's contents. See the next section.

Space that's being used   Space that's free

What's consuming storage

Figure 17-5: Galaxy Tab storage information.

✔ Things that consume the most storage space are videos, music, and pictures, in that order.

✔ To see how much storage space is left, refer to the Available Space item.

✔ Don't bemoan that the Total Space value is far less than the tablet's or media card's capacity. For example, in Figure 17-5, my 16GB media card shows only 14.83GB total space. The missing space is considered overhead, as are several gigabytes taken by the government for tax purposes.

Managing files

You probably didn't get a Galaxy Tab because you enjoy managing files on a computer and wanted to experience the same thrills on a mobile device. Even so, you can manipulate files and folders on your tablet just as you can on a computer. Is there a need to do so? Of course not! But if you want to get dirty with files, you can.

The main tool for managing files is the My Files app, shown in Figure 17-6.

Figure 17-6: The My Files app.

The screen shows features and actions commonly used for file management. If you're into that kind of thing, you'll feel right at home; otherwise I shan't waste your time blathering on about the app, except to say:

- The Storage Stats icon shown in Figure 17-6 may appear differently in the My Files app on the Galaxy Tab 4. In fact, the icon order may change as well, although the app works the same way.

- A shortcut for the My Files app appears in the lower-left corner on the Galaxy Tab S Classic Home screen.

Apps and Widgets

In This Chapter

▶ Placing apps on the Home screen

▶ Working with widgets

▶ Organizing the Home screen

▶ Removing apps

▶ Stopping a crazy app

▶ Organizing the Apps screen

▶ Creating Apps screen folders

At last estimate, over 1.3 million apps are available at the Google Play Store. Why not collect them all?

Okay, perhaps not. But of the apps you do collect, you'll want to keep them neat and tidy. Organization is the keyword, although that does instill a bit of fear. Still, organizing and managing your apps on the Galaxy Tab is a rather painless experience.

Apps and Widgets on the Home Screen

Lots of interesting doodads festoon your tablet's Home screen, like bugs on a windshield after a long trip. The two items you'll notice the most are apps and widgets.

Wonder of Nature
00:00:00 / 00:01:45

✔ The app icons are officially known as *launchers*. Feel free to instead use the term *app icon*.

✔ For the Galaxy Tab S, apps live on the Classic Home screen. See Chapter 3 for more Home screen definitions.

Adding an app to the Home screen

When new apps are installed on your Galaxy Tab, a launcher icon is automatically affixed to the Home screen. You can perform this action manually, which helps put the apps you use most within easy reach. Here's how that works:

1. **View the Home screen page to which you want to add the app launcher icon.**

   The page must have room for the icon. If not, swipe the screen left or right to find another Home screen page.

2. **Tap the Apps icon.**

   You see the Apps screen, home to all the apps on your tablet.

   On the Galaxy Tab 4, ensure that the Apps tab is chosen atop the Apps screen.

3. **Long-press the app icon you want to add to the Home screen.**

   After a moment, the Home screen page you chose in Step 1 appears, similar to what's shown in Figure 18-1.

4. **Drag the app to a position on the Home screen.**

   Launcher icons on the Home screen are aligned to a grid. Other apps may wiggle and jiggle as you find a spot. That's okay.

5. **Lift your finger.**

   Don't worry if the app isn't in the exact spot you want. The later section "Moving icons and widgets" describes how to rearrange icons on the Home screen.

The app hasn't moved: What you see is a *launcher,* which is like a shortcut. You can still find the app on the Apps screen, but now the app is — more conveniently — available on the Home screen.

➔ You can cancel the operation by dragging the icon up to the Cancel item (refer to the upper right in Figure 18-1).

➔ Keep launchers on the Home screen for the apps you use most often.

➔ You can't stuff more icons on the Home screen than will fit in the grid, but the Tab gives you solutions for that crowded situation. One solution is to create an app folder; see the section "Building app folders." A second solution is to add another Home screen page, which is covered in Chapter 19.

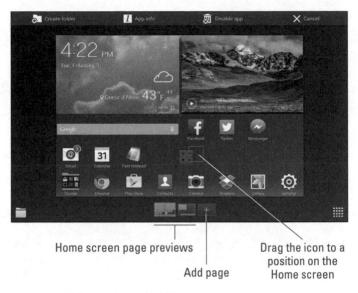

Home screen page previews

Add page

Drag the icon to a
position on the
Home screen

Figure 18-1: Stick an app on the Home screen.

Slapping down widgets

Just as you can add apps to the Home screen, you can also add widgets. A *widget* works like a tiny, interactive or informative window, often providing a gateway into another app on the tablet.

To add a widget to the Home screen, follow these steps on the Galaxy Tab S:

1. **Swipe left or right to view a Home screen page large enough to accommodate the widget.**

   Unlike app launcher icons, widgets come in different sizes.

2. **Long-press a blank part of the Home screen.**

3. **Tap the Widgets icon that appears at the bottom of the screen.**

4. **Swipe through the various pages of widgets to find the one you want.**

   Widgets are listed by name. Below the name is the widget's size relative to the standard launcher icon size. So a 2x2 widget is twice as wide and twice as tall as a launcher icon.

5. **Long-press the widget you want to add.**

6. **Drag the widget to the home screen.**

   Move the widget around to position it. As you drag the widget, existing launcher icons and widgets jiggle to make room.

7. **Lift your finger.**

If the widget grows an orange border, it can be resized. See the next section.

On the Galaxy Tab 4, add widgets by following these steps:

1. **Navigate to the Home screen page where you desire to place the widget.**

2. **Tap the Apps icon.**

3. **Tap the Widget tab atop the Apps screen.**

4. **Continue with Steps 4 through 7 in the preceding set of steps to drag-and-drop the widget on the Home screen.**

After adding some widgets, you may be prompted for additional information, such as a location for a weather widget or a contact name for a contact widget.

- ✔ The variety of available widgets depends on the apps installed. Some apps come with widgets; some don't. Some widgets are independent of any app.

- ✔ Fret not if you change your mind about the widget's location. See the later section, "Moving icons and widgets," for obtaining the proper *feng shui*.

- ✔ To remove a widget, see the section, "Moving icons and widgets."

- ✔ Widgets are added to the Galaxy Tab S Content Home screen similar to the method described in this section. First navigate to the Content Home screen, and then long-press a widget to see the Widgets icon at the bottom of the screen. The widgets available for the Content Home screen aren't as plentiful as those for the Classic Home screen.

Resizing a widget

Some widgets are resizable. You can change a widget's size right after plopping it down on the Home screen, or at any time really: The secret is to long-press the widget. If it grows an orange box, as shown in Figure 18-2, you can change the widget's dimensions.

To resize, drag one of the orange dots in or out. Tap elsewhere on the touchscreen when you've finished resizing.

Moving icons and widgets

Icons and widgets are fastened to the Home screen by something akin to the same glue used on sticky notes. You can easily pick up an icon or a widget, move it around, and then re-stick it. Unlike sticky notes, the icons and widgets never just fall off, or so I'm told.

To move an icon or a widget, long-press it. Eventually, the item seems to lift and break free, as shown in Figure 18-3.

Drag up or down   Drag left or right

Figure 18-2: Adding a widget to the Home screen.

Create an app folder   Long-press to "lift"   Delete icon or widget

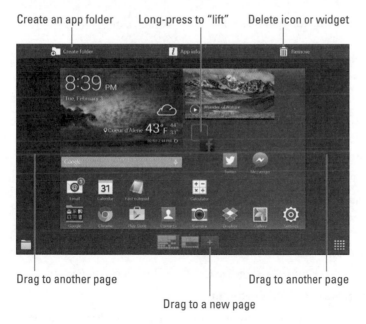

Drag to another page   Drag to another page

Drag to a new page

Figure 18-3: Moving an icon about.

Drag the item to another position on the Home screen. If you drag to the far left or far right of the screen, the icon or widget is sent to another Home screen page.

- ✔ When an icon hovers over the Remove icon, ready to be deleted, its color changes to red.
- ✔ The Create Folder icon, shown in Figure 18-3, is used to create app folders. See the section, "Building app folders."
- ✔ Your clue that an icon or a widget is free and clear to navigate is that the Remove icon appears (refer to Figure 18-3).

Removing an icon or a widget

To banish an icon or a widget from the Home screen, move it to the Remove (trash can) icon that appears on the Home screen. Refer to Figure 18-3 for that icon's location.

- ✔ When the Remove icon turns red, that's your clue that you can lift your finger.
- ✔ Removing an item from the Home screen does not delete the app or widget.
- ✔ See the later section, "Uninstalling apps," for information on uninstalling an app from your Galaxy Tab.

Building app folders

A great way to keep similar apps together on the Home screen is to bundle them into folders. For example, I have a Streaming Music folder on my Tab, along with a Social Networking folder.

To create an app folder, follow these steps:

1. **Long-press an app launcher icon.**

2. **Drag the launcher up to the Create Folder icon atop the screen.**

   Refer to Figure 18-3 for the Create Folder icon's location.

3. **Type a name for the folder.**

   Be short and descriptive, such as Social Networking, Music, or Samsung Stuff I Don't Use.

4. **Touch the OK or Done button to create the newly named folder.**

To add more apps to the folder, drag their launcher icons into the folder: Long-press and icon and move it over the top of the folder icon. Lift your finger to move the app.

App folder icons look different on the Tab S and Tab 4. The Tab 4 uses the traditional Android folder, as shown in Figure 18-4.

Open a folder by touching it. All icons in the folder appear on the touchscreen. Tap an icon to launch that app.

Google   Google

Tab S Folder   Tab 4 Folder

Figure 18-4: Folder icon varieties.

📌 Folder icons are managed just like other icons on the Home screen. You can drag them around by long-pressing them, and you can delete them.

📌 Change a folder's name by opening the folder and then touching the folder's name. Use the onscreen keyboard to type a new folder name.

📌 To remove an icon from a folder, open the folder and drag out the icon.

📌 When the second-to-last last icon is dragged out of a folder, the folder should be removed. If not, drag the last icon out, and then drag the empty folder up to the Remove icon atop the screen.

Manage Your Apps

The good news is that you really don't have to worry about managing apps on your Galaxy Tab. The Android operating system deftly handles that task for you. The bad news is that occasionally you may need to delicately dip your big toe into the app management sea. That's why I wrote this section.

Updating apps

App updates happen all the time. They're automatic. Occasionally you're called upon to perform a manual update. How can you tell? An Updates Available notification appears, looking similar to what's shown in the margin. Here's how to deal with that notification:

1. **Open the Play Store app.**

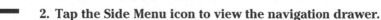

2. **Tap the Side Menu icon to view the navigation drawer.**

   The Side Menu icon appears in the upper-left corner of the screen (and in the margin). You may have to tap the left arrow icon a few times before you can see the Side Menu icon.

3. **Choose My Apps.**

4. **Tap the Update All button.**

5. **If prompted, tap the Accept button to acknowledge the app's permission.**

   You may need to repeat this step for each app in need of an update.

The apps are individually updated. You can view the progress in the Play Store app, or go off and do something else with your Tab.

✔ Yes, you do need an Internet connection to update apps. If the connection is broken, the apps update when the connection is reestablished.

✔ Tap the Stop icon on the My Apps screen to halt the updates.

✔ Most apps are automatically updated; you need not do a thing. The updates do generate a notification icon, shown in the margin. Feel free to dismiss that notification.

Uninstalling an app

I can think of a few reasons to remove an app. It's with eager relish that I remove apps that don't work or somehow annoy me. It's also perfectly okay to remove redundant apps, such as when you have multiple ebook readers that you don't use. Whatever the reason, follow these directions to uninstall an app:

1. **Start the Play Store app.**

2. **Tap the Side Menu icon to view the navigation drawer.**

3. **Choose My Apps.**

4. **Tap the Installed tap and swipe to locate the app that offends you.**

5. **Tap the Uninstall button.**

6. **Touch the OK button to confirm.**

   The app is removed.

The app continues to appear on the All tab on the My Apps screen even after it's been removed. After all, you installed it once.

✔ You can always reinstall paid apps that you've uninstalled. You aren't charged twice for doing so.

✔ You can't remove apps that are preinstalled on the tablet by either Samsung or your cellular provider. I'm sure there's probably a technical way to uninstall the apps, but seriously: Just don't use the apps if you want to remove them and discover that you can't.

✔ One way to avoid apps you don't like is to place them into an Apps screen folder. See the later section, "Working with Apps screen folders."

Choosing a default app

Every so often, you may see the Complete Action Using prompt, similar to the one shown in Figure 18-5.

Multiple apps are available that can deal with your request. You pick one, then choose either Always or Just Once.

Figure 18-5: The Complete Action Using question is posed.

When you choose Always, the same app is always used for whatever action took place: composing email, listening to music, choosing a photo, navigation, and so on.

When you choose Just Once, you see the prompt again and again.

My advice is to choose Just Once until you get sick of seeing the Complete Action Using prompt. At that point, after choosing the same app over and over, choose Always.

The fear, of course, is that you'll make a mistake. Keep reading in the next section.

Clearing default apps

Fret not, gentle reader. The settings you chose for the Complete Action Using prompt can be undone. For example, if you select the Gmail app from Figure 18-5, you can undo that choice by following these steps:

1. **Open the Settings app.**
2. **On the Tab S, tap the Applications tab; on the Tab 4, tap the General tab.**
3. **Choose Default Applications from the left side of the screen.**
4. **Tap the Clear button by the default app.**

   For example, if you Choose Gmail in Figure 18-5, you'd tap the Clear button by the Gmail item.

After you clear the defaults for an app, you will see the Complete Action Using prompt again. The next time you see it, however, make a better choice.

Shutting down an app run amok

It happens. Sometimes an app goes crazy and just won't stop. Although Google tries to keep unstable apps out of the Play Store, not all technology is perfect. If you need to smite an errant app, follow these steps:

1. **Open the Settings app.**

2. **Tap the Applications tab on the Tab S; on the Tab 4 tap the General tab.**

3. **On the left side of the screen, choose Application Manager.**

4. **Swipe right to left to view the Running tab.**

   The Running tab shows only those apps currently running, which includes the crazy app you want to stifle.

5. **Tap the app's entry in the list of running apps.**

6. **Tap the Stop or Force Stop button.**

   If you see a warning, tap the OK button to stop the app.

Only stop an app that you truly cannot stop any other way.

If the app you want to halt appears as a launcher icon on the Home screen, you can pull a shortcut to skip the first five steps in this section: Drag the launcher icon up to the App Info item atop the Home screen. Then you can quickly tap the Stop or Force Stop button.

The problem with randomly quitting an app is that data may get lost or damaged. At the worst, the tablet may become unstable. The only way to fix that situation is to restart the device.

Organizing the Apps Screen

The go-to place for apps on your Galaxy Tab is the Apps screen. It lists all available apps on your tablet, which makes the Apps screen an important place. It's also something you can customize to make accessing your apps easier.

Changing the Apps screen view

The Apps menu sports two views:

>**Customizable Grid:** This view allows app icons to be moved around and organized.

Alphabetical Grid: This view arranges apps in alphabetical order. New apps are inserted into the grid alphabetically. That makes locating an app easier, but it also means the apps change position on the Apps screen each time one is added or removed.

To set the current view, heed these steps:

1. **Tap the Apps icon on the Home screen to visit the Apps screen.**
2. **Tap the Action Overflow icon and choose View Type.**
3. **Select a view, either Customizable Grid or Alphabetical Grid.**

The Apps screen changes to reflect your choice.

Rearranging apps on the Apps screen

The Customizable Grid option for viewing the Apps screen lets you rearrange and order all your phone's apps. Unlike the Alphabetical Grid, the apps stay where you put them.

To begin redecorating the Apps screen, tap the Action Overflow icon and choose the Edit command. The Apps screen enters editing mode. Here are some things you can do:

- Drag an icon to change its position.
- Drag an icon up to the Create Page icon (atop the screen) to add a new Apps screen page.
- Drag an app up to the Uninstall icon (trash) to uninstall that icon.
- Drag an app icon up to the Create Folder icon to build a new Apps screen folder, as described in the next section.

When you've finished editing, tap the Save icon in the upper-right corner of the screen.

New Apps screen pages are created by dragging an app icon over the Create Page icon. To remove a page, simply drag away all of its icons and the page vanishes. (Apps screen pages must have at least one icon.)

Working with Apps screen folders

Just as you can have an apps folder on the Home screen, the Apps screen can sport apps folders. These folders help organize apps on the Apps screen, which may help you locate certain types of apps.

To build an Apps screen folder, follow these steps:

1. Tap the Action Overflow icon and choose Create Folder.

2. Type a name for the folder.

3. Tap the Done or OK button to create the folder.

The folder is created. You'll find it on the far-right Apps screen page. Alas, the folder is empty. To populate it, you need to edit the Apps screen again and drag app icons into the folder.

For example, I created an Apps screen folder that contains pre-installed apps I seldom use. To do so, I built the folder, and then edited the Apps screen to drag those app icons into the folder.

↙ You can work with App screen folder whether the Customizable Grid or Alphabetical Grid view setting is chosen.

↙ Don't forget to tap the Save button atop the screen when you've finished moving app icons into a folder.

↙ To remove an app from a folder, edit the Apps screen and drag the app icon(s) out of the folder.

↙ When a folder is empty, remove it by editing the Apps screen and dragging the folder icon up to the Remove icon atop the screen.

↙ Folders created on the Apps screen can be copied to the Home screen. Drag the folder to the Home screen as you would install any app. See the earlier section, "Adding an app to the Home screen."

19

Customize Your Tab

In This Chapter

▶ Changing the background image

▶ Adding Home screen pages

▶ Setting the screen lock timeout

▶ Customizing the Lock screen

▶ Changing the notification ringtone

▶ Adjusting the brightness

It's entirely possible to own the amazing Galaxy Tab for the rest of your life and never even once bother to customize the gizmo. It's not only possible, it's sad. That's because there exists great potential to make the tablet your own. You can alter so many things, from the way it looks to the way it sounds. The reason for customizing is not simply to change things because you can but to make the tablet work best for how you use it. After all, it's *your* Galaxy tablet.

Home Screen Settings

The Home screen is where the action happens on your Galaxy Tab. To help hone the Home page to meet your demands, several customization options are available. You can change the background image, but more importantly you can add and remove Home screen pages. This section uncovers the secrets.

Hanging new wallpaper

The Home screen has two types of backgrounds, or *wallpapers:* traditional and live. *Live* wallpaper is animated. A not-so-live *(traditional)* wallpaper can be any image, such as a picture you've taken and stored on the tablet.

To set a new wallpaper for the Home screen, obey these steps:

1. **Long-press any empty part of the Home screen.**

   The empty part doesn't have a shortcut icon or widget floating on it.

2. **Tap the Wallpapers icon.**

3. **Choose Home Screen.**

   Choose Home and Lock Screens to set the wallpaper for both locations. (See the later section, "Setting the Lock screen background," for information on the Lock screen's wallpaper.)

4. **Tap a wallpaper to see a preview.**

   Swipe the list left or right to peruse your options. You'll see the preset wallpaper images supplied by Samsung, plus any photos you've used previously as wallpaper. On the far right you'll find the live wallpapers.

5. **Tap the Set Wallpaper button to confirm your choice.**

   The new wallpaper takes over the Home screen.

If you prefer to use an image from the tablet's photo library, tap the More Images button in Step 4. Choose an image. Crop the image by manipulating the cropping rectangle on the screen. Tap the Done button to set the wallpaper.

The steps in this section work differently on the Galaxy Tab 4: Long-press the screen and choose the Set Wallpaper action. Choose the Home Screen option, and then select a source:

Wallpapers: Choose a preset wallpaper.

Live Wallpapers: Select an animated Home screen background.

Gallery, Photos, and other apps: Choose one of your own images.

When choosing your own image, you'll be asked to crop. Tap the Set Wallpaper button to assign the image as your tablet's Home screen background.

✔ Be careful how you crop the wallpaper image when you choose one of your own photos. When both Home and Lock screens are chosen, zoom out (pinch your fingers on the touchscreen) to ensure that the entire image is cropped properly for both horizontal and vertical orientations.

✔ Live wallpapers can be obtained from the Google Play Store. See Chapter 15.

✔ The Zedge app is an über-repository of wallpaper images, collected from Android users all over the world. Zedge is free at the Google Play Store.

✔ See Chapter 12 for more information about the Gallery app, including details on how to crop an image.

Managing Home screen pages

How many pages can you find on the Home screen? My Galaxy Tab S shipped with only two pages (on the Classic Home screen). My Galaxy Tab 4 also shows only two. That is by no means the limit.

To add another Home screen page on the Galaxy Tab S, follow these steps:

1. **Long-press a blank part of the Home screen.**

2. **Swipe the screen right to left until you see the screen with the large plus on it.**

   If you don't see the Plus icon, you can't add more Home screen pages.

3. **Tap the Plus icon.**

   The new page appears, empty and ready for more icons and widgets.

4. **Press the Back button to end Home screen editing.**

On the Galaxy Tab 4, follow these steps to add another Home screen page:

1. **Pinch the Home screen.**

   You see a Home screen page overview, similar to what's shown in Figure 19-1.

2. **Tap the Plus icon to add another page.**

3. **Press the Back button when you're done.**

If you don't like the Home screen page's position, move a page: Edit the Home screen (Step 1 for both types of Tab), and then long-press a page to drag it to a new position.

To remove a Home screen page, edit the Home screen: On the Galaxy Tab S, long-press a blank part of the Home screen; on the Tab 4, pinch the Home screen. Drag an unwanted page up to the Remove icon at the top of the screen. If the page has icons and widgets on it, you'll be asked to confirm.

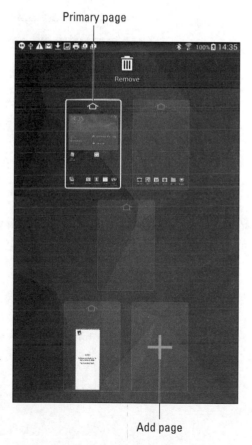

Primary page

Add page

Figure 19-1: Manipulating Home screen panels on the Tab 4.

The wee Home icon on the page previews (refer to Figure 19-1) indicates the primary Home screen page. Tap the icon on a specific page to set it as the primary page. It's the page you'll see when viewing the Home screen and when you press the tablet's Home button.

There's no way to undo a Home screen panel deletion. You have to add a new blank panel and then repopulate it with icons and widgets.

Adjusting the screen timeout

You can manually lock your Galaxy Tab at any time by pressing the Power Lock key. That's why it's called the Power *Lock* key. When you don't manually lock the tablet, it automatically locks itself after a given period of inactivity.

You have control over the automatic lock timeout value, which can be set from 15 seconds to several minutes. Obey these steps:

1. **Open the Settings app.**
2. **Tap the Device tab, and choose Display from the left side of the screen.**
3. **On the right side of the screen, choose Screen Timeout.**
4. **Select a timeout value from the list.**

   I prefer 10 minutes. The standard value is 30 seconds.

The Screen Timeout measures inactivity; when you don't touch the screen or tap an icon or a button, the timer starts ticking. About 5 seconds before the timeout value you set (in Step 4), the touchscreen dims. Then it turns off, and the tablet locks. If you touch the screen before then, the timer is reset.

The Lock screen has its own timeout. If you unlock the tablet but don't work the screen lock, the tablet locks itself automatically after about 10 seconds.

Lock Screen Configuration

The Lock screen is different from the Home screen, although the two locations share similar traits. As with the Home screen, you can customize the Lock screen. You can change the background, add app launcher shortcuts and info cards, and do all sorts of tricks.

For information on setting screen locks, refer to Chapter 20.

Setting the Lock screen background

The Lock screen wallpaper can be the same image as the Home screen or different. You can set the image as described in the earlier section, "Hanging new wallpaper," or you can follow these steps:

1. **Open the Settings app.**

2. **Tap the Device tab, and then choose the Wallpaper category from the left side of the screen.**

3. **Choose Lock Screen on the right side of the screen.**

4. **Select a wallpaper from the scrolling list at the bottom of the screen.**

   Tap the More Images item to choose an image from the tablet's photo library. You will need to crop the image before setting it.

5. **Tap the Set Wallpaper or Done button to apply the image.**

For the Galaxy Tab 4, work Steps 1 through 3, then choose a wallpaper type from the items displayed: Gallery, Travel Wallpaper, and Wallpapers.

✔ Unlike the Home screen, Live Wallpaper cannot be applied to the Lock screen.

✔ Travel Wallpaper is a special Lock screen wallpaper option. When selected, the tablet downloads images for "travel recommendations" to use as the Lock screen wallpaper.

Adding Lock screen shortcuts

When the Swipe screen lock is set, you have the option of placing up to five app launcher icons on the Lock screen. You can use these Lock screen short-cuts to both unlock the tablet and immediately start the app: Simply swipe the app launcher icon on the Lock screen.

For example, to unlock the tablet and instantly use its camera, swipe the Camera app icon when you unlock your Tab.

To configure Lock screen shortcuts, heed these steps:

1. **Open the Settings app.**

2. **Tap the Device tab, and then choose Lock Screen from the left side of the screen.**

3. **On the right side of the screen, slide the Shortcuts Master Control to the on position.**

The Master Control is green when it's on.

4. **Tap the Shortcuts item.**

You see the icons that will appear on the Lock screen.

To add another icon, tap the Plus icon, shown in Figure 19-2. Choose an app to add to the list.

To remove an app, long-press it and drag it down to the Delete icon at the bottom of the screen.

Master Control

✔ A maximum of five Lock screen shortcuts can be selected. You can have fewer, if you like. One is the minimum.

Figure 19-2: Managing Lock screen shortcuts.

✔ Lock screen shortcuts appear only when the Swipe screen lock is chosen. See Chapter 20 for information on setting screen locks.

Displaying Lock screen cards

You can configure the Galaxy Tab S to show up-to-date information on the Lock screen. This information appears in the form of a scrolling list of cards across the bottom of the screen, similar to those shown in Figure 19-3.

To activate the Lock screen cards, follow these directions:

1. **Open the Settings app.**

2. **Tap the Device tab, and choose Lock Screen from the left side of the window.**

3. **Choose Lock Screen Card.**

4. **Place a green check mark by the cards that you want to appear on the Lock screen.**

To disable this feature, uncheck all the items.

You can simply admire the cards, or you can take advantage of their information: Tap a card, such as the new email card, and then unlock the tablet. The app associated with the card opens so you can view additional information.

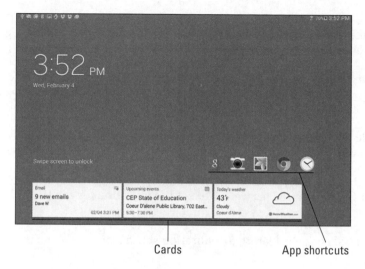

Cards   App shortcuts

Figure 19-3: Lock screen cards.

Various Galactic Adjustments

You have plenty of things to adjust, tune, and tweak on your Galaxy Tab. The Settings app is the gateway to all these options, and I'm sure you could waste hours there if you had hours to waste. My guess is that your time is precious; therefore, this section highlights some of the more worthy options and settings.

Singing a different tune

The Sound screen is where you control which sound the tablet plays as a ringtone, but it's also where you can set volume and vibration options.

To display the Sound screen, tap the Device tab and choose Sound from the left side of the screen.

Here are the worthy options on the Sound screen:

Notifications: Choose which sound you want to hear for a notification alert. Tap Notifications, choose a sound, and then tap OK. Or to have no notification sounds, choose the Silent option.

✔ If you have a sound app installed on your Tab, you may see a Complete Action Using prompt. Choose Media Storage to select Galaxy Tab sounds; choose the other app to use it as a sound source. Also see Chapter 18 for information on the Complete Action Using prompt.

✔ Also check individual apps for their own notification sounds. For example, Facebook and Twitter set their sounds by using the Settings action in those individual apps.

Touch Sounds: Set this item on if you prefer that the tablet provide audible feedback when you touch the screen. Alas, you cannot alter the *poit* sound made when the Touch Sounds setting is active.

Haptic Feedback: This item activates a wee bit of vibration when touching some items on the screen or the navigation buttons (Recent and Back).

Vibration Intensity: Use this item to adjust how vigorously the tablet vibrates when muted, as well as to set the vibration for the Haptic Feedback setting.

Not all Galaxy Tabs feature the vibration settings.

Changing visual settings

Probably the key thing you want to adjust visually on your Galaxy Tab is the screen's brightness. To set how bright or dim the touchscreen appears, follow these steps:

1. **Open the Settings app.**

2. **Choose the Device tab, and then choose Display from the left side of the screen.**

3. **Choose Brightness.**

4. **Adjust the brightness slider.**

   Left is dim; right is bright.

5. **Tap the OK button to set the tablet's screen intensity.**

Tap Auto box to have the tablet automatically adjust its brightness based on the ambient light. This setting isn't available on all Tabs.

✔ A shortcut to setting the brightness can be found in the Notifications list, just below the Quick Settings.

✔ The screen timeout is also considered a visual setting. Refer to the earlier section, "Adjusting the screen timeout."

✔ See Chapter 3 for more information on Quick Settings.

20

Galactic Security

In This Chapter

▶ Locating the various screen locks

▶ Setting a screen lock

▶ Using the fingerprint screen lock

▶ Setting owner info text

▶ Encrypting the tablet's data

▶ Creating separate user accounts

▶ Adding a kids account

*A*s a citizen of the twenty-first century, you no doubt have an extensive digital presence. This includes accounts, passwords, perhaps even financial information — and you tote around access to that information, if not the information itself, with your Galaxy Tab everywhere you go. Obviously, security is going to be an issue. Don't take it too lightly.

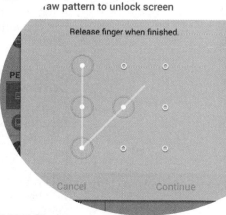

Lock Your Tablet

If you keep anything important on your Galaxy Tab, or when you have multiple users on the same tablet or a corporate email account, you need Lock screen security. And I'm referring to more security than the simple Swipe screen lock.

Finding the screen locks

Lock screen security is set from the Select Screen Lock screen. Here's how to get there:

1. **Open the Settings app.**

2. **Tap the Device tab and choose Lock Screen from the left side of the screen.**

3. **On the right side of the screen, choose Screen Lock.**

4. **Work any existing screen lock to continue.**

   When the Swipe or None lock is set, you just see the Select Screen Lock screen.

Several locks are shown on the Select Screen Lock screen. They are

- **Swipe:** Unlock the tablet by swiping your finger across the screen.
- **Pattern:** Trace a pattern on the touchscreen to unlock the tablet.
- **Fingerprint:** Swipe your finger over the Home button to gain access to the tablet. This option isn't available on all Galaxy Tabs.
- **PIN:** Unlock the tablet by typing a personal identification number (PIN).
- **Password:** Type a password to unlock the tablet.
- **None:** The screen doesn't lock.

The most secure locks are PIN and Password. The Pattern and Fingerprint locks come in second, but they require a PIN or a password as backup. The Swipe and None locks are considered nonsecure.

Removing the screen lock

You use the Screen Lock window not only to place a lock on the tablet but also to remove locks.

After visiting the Screen Lock window, as described in the preceding section, you can choose the None option to remove all screen locks. To restore the original screen lock, choose Swipe.

Setting a PIN

Perhaps the most common and the second most secure method of locking the tablet is to use a PIN, or personal identification number. This type of screen lock is also employed as a backup for less-secure screen unlocking methods.

A *PIN lock* is a code between 4 and 16 numbers long. It contains only numbers, 0 through 9. To set a PIN lock, follow the directions in the earlier section "Finding the screen locks" to reach the Set Screen Lock window. Choose PIN from the list of locks.

Use the onscreen keypad to type your PIN once, and tap the Continue button. Type the PIN again to confirm that you know it. Tap OK. The next time you turn on or wake up the tablet, you'll need to type that PIN to get access.

To disable the PIN, reset the security level as described in the preceding section.

I know of no recovery method available should you forget your tablet's PIN. Don't forget it!

Assigning a password

The most secure — and therefore the most arduous — screen lock is a full-on password. Unlike a PIN (refer to the preceding section), a *password* can contain numbers, symbols, and both uppercase and lowercase letters.

Set a password by choosing Password from the Screen Lock window; refer to the earlier section "Finding the screen locks" for information on getting to that screen. The password you select must be at least four characters long. Longer passwords are more secure.

You're prompted to type the password whenever you unlock the tablet or when you try to change the screen lock. Touch the OK button to accept the password you've typed.

You're out of luck should you forget the Tab's password.

Creating an unlock pattern

One of the most common ways to lock a Galaxy tablet is to apply an *unlock pattern.* The pattern must be traced exactly as it was created to unlock the device and get access to your apps and other tablet features.

1. **Summon the Screen Lock window.**

   Refer to the earlier section "Finding the screen locks."

2. **Choose Pattern.**

   If you've not yet set a pattern lock, you may see a tutorial describing the process; touch the Next button to skip over the dreary directions.

3. **Trace an unlock pattern.**

   Use Figure 20-1 as your inspiration. You can trace over the dots in any order, but you can trace over a dot only once. The pattern must cover at least four dots.

4. **Touch the Continue button.**

5. **Redraw the pattern.**

   You need to prove to the doubtful tablet that you know the pattern.

6. **Touch the Confirm button.**

7. Type a PIN to back up the pattern lock in case you forget.

Specific details on setting a PIN lock are found earlier in this chapter.

And the pattern lock is set.

To ensure that the pattern shows up, check that the Make Pattern Visible option is selected on the Lock Screen window. For even more security, you can deselect the option, but you have to be sure to remember how — and where — the pattern goes.

- The unlock pattern can be as simple or as complex as you like. I'm a big fan of simple.

- Wash your hands! Smudge marks on the display can betray your pattern.

Unlocking the tablet with your finger

The Galaxy Tab S features a fingerprint scanner, nestled in the Home button. Use that scanner to unlock your Tab with a swipe of your finger. Here's how to set it up:

I began the pattern here   Keep tracing

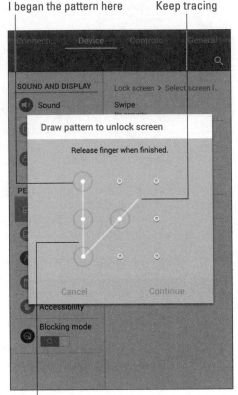

Pattern so far

Figure 20-1: Setting an unlock pattern.

1. Get to the Select Screen Lock screen.

Refer to the earlier section "Finding the screen locks" for specific directions.

2. Choose Fingerprint.

Directions may appear on the screen, which you are free not to read. Tap the OK button to dismiss them.

3. Choose your favorite digit or hallux, and swipe it over the animated dots on the screen, as well as the Home button.

A countdown appears on the screen. You must repeat this step so that the fingerprint is properly registered.

4. Repeat Step 3 as required.

5. **Type a password and confirm.**

   The password is a backup, most likely in case you get your finger chopped off.

The Tab is now ready to be unlocked by using your fingerprint.

The fingerprint you set stays registered with the tablet, even when you switch to another screen lock.

Other Tablet Security

Locking your tablet with a secure screen lock works wonders as far as keeping your tablet's information safe. The screen lock doesn't help, however, should your tablet get lost or stolen. That's when more tools are required for a swift recovery.

Adding owner info text

If your Galaxy Tab someday gets lost, it would be nice if a good Samaritan found it. What would be even more helpful is if you had some information on the Lock screen to help that kind person find you and return your Tab.

Follow these steps to add owner information text to the Lock screen:

1. **Visit the Settings app.**
2. **Tap the Device tab, and then choose Lock Screen from the categories on the left side of the screen.**
3. **On the right side of the screen, choose Owner Information.**

4. **Type text in the box.**

   You can type more than one line of text, though the information is displayed on the Lock screen as a single line.
5. **Ensure that the Show Owner Info on Lock Screen option is selected.**
6. **Tap the OK button.**

Whatever text you type in the box appears on the Lock screen. Therefore, I recommend typing something useful, as the command suggests: your name, phone number, and email address, for example. This way, should you lose your tablet and an honest person finds it, that person can get it back to you.

Find your lost tablet

Someday, you may lose your beloved Galaxy Tab. It might be for a few panic-filled seconds, or it might be for forever. The hardware solution is to weld a heavy object to the tablet, such as an anvil or a rhinoceros, but that strategy kind of defeats the entire mobile/wireless paradigm. (Well, not so much the rhino.) The software solution is to use a cell phone locator service.

Samsung's solution is to use their Find My Mobile service. You need a Samsung account to activate this feature. Whether you have one or not, visit the signup page by following these steps:

1. **Open the Settings app.**

2. **Tap the General tab, and then choose Security from the left side of the screen.**

3. **On the right side of the screen, tap Go to Website.**

   The tablet's web browser app opens and visits the Find My Mobile page on Samsung's website. You can log in or tap the Sign Up link to set up your Samsung account.

Once activated, use the Remote Controls item on the Setting app's Security screen to enable remote controls. If you tablet gets lost or stolen, you can use any tablet or computer to log into your Samsung account and remotely control the device, which includes wiping all the data.

✔ All "lost phone/tablet" apps work the same: They coordinate between your device and a website. Should anything happen to your mobile gizmo, you use the website to remotely access it.

✔ If you don't want a Samsung account, alternative Find My Tablet apps are available at the Google Play Store. One that I use is Lookout Mobile Security. Try the free version to see whether or not you like the app. If so, get the paid version, which offers more and better features.

Avoiding Android viruses

I often get asked about antivirus security software for the Galaxy Tab. The requests probably come from the PC world, where viruses are real and deadly and all-too-frequent. Fortunately, such isn't the case on your Tab.

Although evil and malicious apps do exist, keep in mind that they don't advertise themselves as such. The key to knowing whether an app is evil is to look at its description. For example, if a simple grocery-list app uses tablet's mobile data signal and the app doesn't need to access the Internet, it's suspect.

In the history of the Android operating system, only a handful of malicious apps have been distributed, and most of them were found in Asia. Google routinely removes these apps from the Play Store, and a feature of the Android operating system even lets Google remove apps from your phone. So, you're pretty safe.

Generally speaking, avoid "hacker" apps, porn, and those apps that use social engineering to make you do things on your Galaxy Tab that you wouldn't otherwise do, such as remove your screen lock or volunteer personal information.

Encrypting your Tab

When the information on your galactic tablet must be really, really secure, you can take the drastic step to encrypting its internal and external storage. For most Tab uses, this step is a bit much. However, if you're using your Galaxy Tab to store plans for the Death Star, you might want to consider it.

Start by applying a secure screen lock. Only the Password lock is acceptable. The password must be at least six characters long and contain at least one number.

Second, ensure that the tablet is either plugged in or fully charged. Encryption takes a while and you don't want the Tab pooping out before the process is complete.

Third, follow these steps to encrypt your tablet's internal storage:

1. **Open the Settings app.**
2. **Tap the General Tab and choose the Security item.**
3. **On the right side of the screen, choose Encrypt Device.**

    If you haven't followed my advice in this this section, you'll need to charge the tablet or set a password or both.

4. **Tap the Encrypt Device button.**
5. **Wait.**

You can choose the item Encrypt External SD Card to perform the same operation on its storage as well.

After the Tab is encrypted, only by unlocking it with the given password will anyone be able to access its storage.

My advice is not to encrypt your tablet but instead use a strong password. Adding remote security, as described in the preceding section, is also a good idea.

Performing a factory data reset

The most secure thing you can do with your information on the Galaxy Tab is to erase it all. The procedure is known as a factory data reset. It effectively restores the Tab back to its original state, as you received the device after opening the box.

A factory data reset is a drastic thing. It not only removes all information from storage but also erases all your accounts. Don't take this step lightly! In fact, if you're using this procedure to cure some ill, I recommend first getting support.

When you're ready to erase all the tablet's data, follow these steps:

1. **Start the Settings app.**

2. **Tap the General tab, and then select Backup and Reset from the left side of the screen.**

3. **Choose Factory Data Reset.**

4. **Touch the Reset Device button.**

5. **If prompted, work the screen lock.**

   This level of security prevents others from idly messing with your Tab.

6. **Touch the Delete All button to confirm.**

   All the information you've set or stored on the tablet is purged, including all your accounts, any apps you've downloaded, music, everything.

 Practical instances when this action is necessary include selling your tablet or giving it to someone else to use. That's the perfect time to perform a factory data reset.

It's Everyone's Tab!

Computers have long had the capability to allow multiple users on the same device. Each person has his own account and customized items in his account. It's a good idea for a computer, but for a tablet?

Your Galaxy Tab can sport several users. While I would suggest that each person get his own Tab (and his own copy of this book), that's not always practical. A better solution is to give all the folks, including the kiddies, their own user account on the device.

Adding another user

When someone else desires to use your Galaxy Tab, don't just hand it over! Instead, create a custom user account for that person.

First, apply a screen lock to your account on the Tab. See the earlier section, "Lock Your Tablet." Ensure that the screen lock is at least medium security; PIN or Password locks are preferred.

Second, get together with the other human and follow these steps:

1. **Open the Settings app.**

2. **Tap the Device tab, and then choose Users from the left side of the screen.**

   On the Galaxy Tab 4, the Users item is found on the General tab.

3. **Tap the Add icon.**

The icon looks like a big plus and is found in the upper-right corner of the screen.

4. **Choose User.**

See the later section "Configuring the Tab for a kid's account" for information on the Restricted Profile account type.

5. **Tap the OK button after ignoring the Add User info.**

6. **Tap the Set Up Now button, and then hand the Tab over to the other person so that he can continue configuring the device.**

At this point, the other person configures the Galaxy Tab exactly as you did when you first set up your account. He'll specify a Google/Gmail account and set other options, and then he can start using the tablet. All his settings, apps, email, and other items are unique to his account. And he cannot access your account unless he knows how to work your screen lock.

✓ I recommend that each user on the Tab have an account protected with a medium- to high-security screen lock.

✓ The tablet's first user (most likely you) is the main user, the one who has primary administrative control.

✓ Remove an account by following Steps 1 through 4 in this section. Tap the account you want to remove, and then tap the Delete (trash can) icon. Touch the OK or Delete button to confirm.

Switching users

Multiple accounts on your Galaxy Tab appear in the upper-right corner of the Lock screen. The current account is shown as a bubble. To select another account, tap the triangle, as illustrated in Figure 20-2. Choose the account from the list, then work the Lock screen to gain access.

When you've finished using the tablet, lock the screen. Other users can then access their own accounts as described in this section.

Configuring the Tab for a kid's account

Don't just hand over your Galaxy Tab to peanut! Craft a kid's account for him to use. That way,

Current account

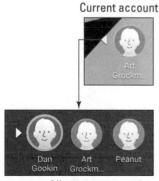

All accounts

Figure 20-2: Choosing an account on the Lock screen.

you can set which apps he can or cannot use, as well as prevent him from downloading millions of dollars of apps, music, and video.

To add a kid's account, follow the steps in the earlier section, "Adding another user." Choose the Restricted Profile account type. Yes, you'll need to apply a secure screen lock to your own account before you add the kid's account.

After creating the account, you'll see the Application/Content Restrictions screen. Here's what to do next:

1. **Tap the account name, New Restricted Account, to replace it with your child's name — or whatever name he chooses.**

2. **Place a check mark by the Location Access item if you want his location tracked as he uses the tablet.**

   Most parents prefer to keep this item unchecked.

3. **Swipe through the list of programs and place a check mark by the ones you would allow your wee one to use.**

   These would include various games or whatever other apps you deem appropriate. Some apps, such as Google, Netflix, and Play Movies & TV, feature a Settings icon. Tap that icon to make further adjustments, such as determining what level of entertainment would be appropriate for your child.

See the preceding section for information on switching to the kid's account.

Taking the Galaxy with You

*L*ast time I checked, the Galaxy Tab didn't have a rolling tread, like a tank. That would be nifty, and I'm sure that more Real Men would buy a Tab with a tank tread, but that's not my point: Your tablet is a mobile device. It's wireless. It runs on battery power. You can take the Galaxy Tab with you everywhere you go and not get those peculiar looks you get when you take the washing machine with you.

How far can you go with your Tab? As far as you want. As long as you can carry the tablet with you, it goes where you go. How it functions may change depending on your environment.

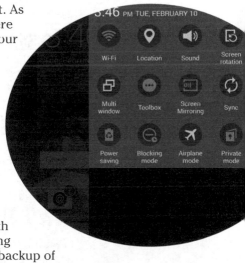

Before You Go

Unless the house is on fire, you should prepare several things before leaving on a trip with your Galactic tablet. First and most important, of course, is to charge the thing. I plug my tablet in overnight when I'm leaving the next day.

Another good thing to do is to synchronize media with your computer. This operation isn't so much for taking media with you but rather to ensure that you have a backup of the tablet's media on your computer. See Chapter 17 for synchronization information.

Consider getting some ebooks and music for the road. I prefer to sit and stew over the Play Books online library before I leave, as opposed to wandering aimlessly in some airport sundry store, trying hard to focus on the good books rather than on the salty snacks. Chapter 14 covers reading ebooks on your Galaxy Tab.

Also — and this is important: Remember to download ebooks and music, especially if you'll be somewhere that the Internet is unavailable. Chapter 15 offers information on keeping these items on your Tab.

Another nifty thing to do is to save some web pages for later reading. I usually start my day by perusing online articles and angry letters to the editor in my local paper. Because I don't have time to read that stuff before I leave, and I do have time on the plane and I'm extremely unwilling to pay for in-flight Wi-Fi, I save my favorite websites for later reading. Here's how to save a web page by using the Internet app:

1. **Navigate to the page you want to save for later reading.**

2. **Tap the Action Overflow icon and choose Save Page.**

    The page is downloaded, saved to the tablet's internal storage.

Repeat these steps for each web page you want to read when offline.

To view the page, touch the Bookmarks icon, and then touch the Saved Pages tab or choose Saved Pages from the action bar. You see the web page listed, along with other items you've downloaded.

For an airplane jaunt that lasts longer than 10 minutes, load up your Tab with plenty of games. Sure, you can convince yourself that you really, really are going to get some work done during your flight. You may have even promised the boss, but games really do help make the time pass quickly.

Finally, don't forget your tickets! Many airlines offer apps that may traveling easy because they generate notifications for your schedule and provide timely gate changes or flight delays. Plus, you can use the Tab as your eticket. Search the Play Store to see whether your preferred airline offers an app.

Galaxy Tab Travel Tips

I'm not a frequent flier, but I am a nerd. The most amount of junk I've carried with me on a flight is two laptop computers and three smartphones. I know that's not a record, but it's enough to warrant my list of travel tips, all of which apply to taking the Galaxy Tab with you on an extended journey:

✔ Bring the tablet's AC adapter and USB cable with you. Put them in your carry-on luggage. Many airports feature USB chargers, so you can charge the tablet in an airport if you need to.

✔ At the security checkpoint, place your tablet in a bin by itself or with other electronics. If you're TSA-Pre (pre-checked through security), you don't have to put the Tab in its own bin, but check with the TSA agents to confirm.

✔ Scan for the airport's Wi-Fi service. Most airports don't charge for the service, although you may have to agree to terms by using the tablet's web browser app to visit the airport's website.

Into the Wild Blue Yonder

It truly is the most trendy of things to be aloft with the latest mobile gizmo. Like taking a smartphone on a plane, however, you have to follow some rules.

The good news is that because your Galaxy Tab isn't a smartphone, you can leave it on for the duration of the flight. All you need to do is place the tablet into Airplane mode. Follow these steps just before takeoff:

1. **Open the Settings app.**

2. **Tap the Connections tab.**

3. **Slide the Master Control by the Airplane Mode item to the on position.**

   Green is on.

4. **Touch the OK button if prompted.**

   The tablet turns off its Wi-Fi and Bluetooth radios.

 While the tablet is in Airplane mode, a special icon appears in the status area at the top of the screen.

 And now, for the shortcut: To put the Galaxy tablet into Airplane mode, press and hold down the Power button and choose the Airplane Mode command.

Oh! Another secret: Pull down the notifications shade and touch the Airplane Mode Quick Setting. You may need to tap the View All Quick Settings icon to find that Quick Settings, as shown in Figure 21-1.

By the way, you can reactivate Wi-Fi while the tablet is in Airplane mode. It's okay to do so, especially when in-flight Wi-Fi is available. Some airlines offer that service free, but for others you have to overpay.

Airplane Mode Quick Setting   View all/view row

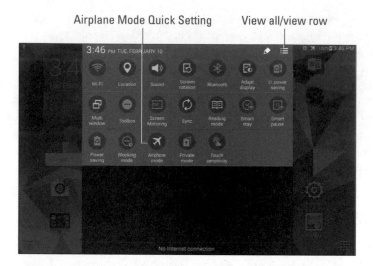

Figure 21-1: Finding the Airplane Mode Quick Setting.

To exit Airplane mode, repeat the steps in this section but remove the green check mark by touching the square next to Airplane Mode.

- ✔ When inflight Wi-Fi isn't available, consider downloading ebooks, music, and web pages to your Tab. Refer to the section, "Before You Go," earlier in this chapter.

- ✔ You can still compose email while the tablet is in Airplane mode. The messages aren't sent until an Internet connection is again established.

- ✔ Airplane mode disables the tablet's Bluetooth radio and GPS. If you have an LTE Tab, its mobile data radio is also disabled.

The Galaxy Goes Abroad

Have no worries taking your Galaxy Tab abroad. The Wi-Fi Tab most definitely can use any Wi-Fi Internet access available. The LTE Tab might be able to use the mobile data network at your location, although you should take some precautions. After all, you don't want to incur data-roaming charges, especially when they're priced in *zloty* or *pengö*.

Traveling overseas with the tablet

The Galaxy Tab works great overseas. The two resources you need to heed are a way to recharge the battery and a way to access Wi-Fi. As long as you have both of them, you're pretty much set. (Data roaming is covered in the next section.)

The tablet's AC plug can easily plug into a foreign wall socket, which allows you to charge the tablet in outer Wamboolistan. I charged my tablet nightly while I spent time in France, and it worked like a charm. All you need is an adapter. You don't need a transformer or a power converter, just the dongle that allows you to plug into a wall socket. That's it. You're good.

Wi-Fi is pretty universal, and as long as your location offers this service, you can connect the tablet and pick up your email, browse the web, or do whatever other Internet activities you desire. Even if you have to pay for Wi-Fi access, I believe that you'll find it less expensive than paying a data-roaming charge.

   ✔ If you want to use Skype for placing an overseas phone call, you need to set up Skype credit. See Chapter 7 for more information on making Skype calls.

   ✔ Many overseas hotels and B&Bs offer free Wi-Fi. When your hotel doesn't, visit an Internet café. These locations are far more numerous in countries outside the US, and the access is reasonably priced.

Disabling mobile data and data roaming

When I've taken my cellular Galaxy Tab abroad, I've kept it in Airplane mode. If you do that, there's no chance of data-roaming charges. Simply use the tablet's Wi-Fi for Internet access.

Just to be sure that your Tab doesn't latch onto a foreign cellular service and, say, download 80GB of app updates (not that my Tab has ever done such a thing), consider disabling mobile data. Heed these steps:

1. **Open the Settings app.**

2. **Tap the Connection tab and choose More Networks from the left side of the screen.**

3. **On the right side of the screen, choose Mobile Networks.**

4. **Remove the check mark by the option Mobile Data.**

   And you're good to go — literally.

Of course, you don't need to disable mobile data or keep the tablet stuck in Airplane mode. You can simply wait for your data bill's arrival in the mail. I prefer not to have such a surprise.

✔ Before you travel abroad, contact your cellular provider and ask about overseas data roaming. A subscription service or other options may be available, especially when you plan to stay overseas for an extended length of time.

✔ If you do get an overseas subscription, repeat the steps in this section and most definitely remove the check mark (if it's there) by the Data Roaming option. You don't want the tablet to be roaming overseas.

✔ With the tablet's mobile data disabled, you have to rely entirely upon Wi-Fi for Internet access. See Chapter 16.

22

Maintenance and Troubleshooting

In This Chapter

▶ Cleaning the tablet

▶ Checking the battery

▶ Saving battery power

▶ Solving annoying problems

▶ Searching for support

▶ Troubleshooting issues

▶ Getting answers

I hear that the maintenance on the Eiffel Tower is arduous. Once a year, the French utterly disassemble the landmark; individually scrub every girder, nut, and bolt; and then put it all back together. The entire operation is performed early in the morning, so when Paris wakes up, no one notices. Well, people notice that the Tower is cleaner, but no one notices that it was completely disassembled, cleaned, and rebuilt. Truly, the French are amazing.

Fortunately, maintenance for your Galaxy Tab isn't as consuming as maintenance on one of the world's great monuments. For example, cleaning the tablet takes mere seconds, and no disassembly is required. It's cinchy! Beyond covering maintenance, this chapter offers suggestions for using the battery, plus it gives you some helpful tips and Q&A.

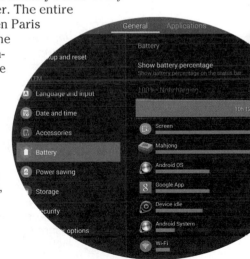

Regular Galactic Maintenance

Relax. Maintenance for your Galaxy Tab is simple and quick. Basically, I can summarize it in three words: Keep it clean. Beyond that, another task worthy of attention is backing up the information stored on your tablet.

Keeping it clean

You probably already keep your tablet clean. Perhaps you're one of those people who use their sleeves to wipe the touchscreen. Of course, better than your sleeve is something called a *microfiber cloth*. This item can be found at any computer- or office-supply store.

✔ Never clean the touchscreen by using a liquid — especially ammonia or alcohol. Those substances damage the touchscreen, rendering it unable to read your input. Further, such harsh chemicals can smudge the display, making it more difficult to see.

✔ If the screen keeps getting dirty, consider adding a screen protector. This specially designed cover prevents the screen from getting scratched or dirty while also letting you use your finger on the touchscreen. Be sure that the screen protector is designed for use with your Samsung Galaxy tablet model.

Backing up your stuff

A *backup* is a safety copy of information. For your tablet, the backup copy includes contact information, music, photos, video, and apps, plus any settings you've made to customize your tablet. Copying that information to another source is one way to keep the information safe in case anything happens to your Galaxy Tab.

Yes, a backup is a good thing. Lamentably, there's no universal method of backing up the stuff on a tablet.

Your Google account information is backed up automatically. That information includes the tablet's address book, Gmail inbox, calendar appointments, and any apps you've obtained as well as other Play Store purchases. Because that information automatically syncs with the Internet, a backup is always present.

To confirm that your Google account information is being backed up, heed these steps:

1. **Open the Settings app.**

2. **Tap the General Tab, and then choose Accounts.**

3. **On the right side of the screen, choose your Google account.**

4. **Tap your Gmail address.**

5. **Ensure that check marks appear by every item in the list.**

   These are the items that synchronize between the tablet and your Google account on the Internet.

   You're not done yet!

6. **On the left side of the screen, choose the Backup and Reset item.**

7. **Ensure that both items shown on the right side of the screen have green check marks.**

   There. Now you can rest easy.

Beyond your Google account, which is automatically backed up, the rest of the information can be manually backed up. You can synchronize information on the tablet with your computer by using an app such as Dropbox, or you can manually copy files from the tablet's internal storage to the computer as a form of backup. These topics are covered in Chapter 17.

Yes, I agree: Manual backup isn't an example of technology making your life easier.

Updating the system

Every so often, a new version of the Android operating system becomes available. It's an *Android* update because Android is the name of the operating system, not because your Galaxy Tab thinks that it's some type of robot.

When an automatic update occurs, you see an alert or a message, indicating that a system upgrade is available. The message may be as subtle as a notification icon, or it might be a card onscreen informing you that an update is necessary. My advice: Install the update and get it over with. Don't dally.

✔ If possible, connect the tablet to a power source during a software update. You don't want the battery to die in the middle of the operation.

✔ You can check for updates manually: In the Settings app, tap the General tab and select About Device on the left side of the screen. Tap the Software Update action. When the system is up-to-date (which is about 99.99 percent of the time), the screen tells you so. Otherwise, you find directions for updating the Android operating system.

✔ Non-Android system updates might also be issued. For example, Samsung may send an update to the Galaxy Tab's guts. This type of update is often called a *firmware* update. As with Android updates, my advice is to accept all firmware updates.

Battery Care and Feeding

Perhaps the most important item you can monitor and maintain on your Galaxy Tab is its battery. The battery supplies the necessary electrical juice by which the device operates. Without battery power, your tablet is basically an expensive trivet. Keep an eye on the battery.

Monitoring the battery

You can find information about the Galaxy tablet's battery status in the upper-right corner of the screen, next to the current time in the status area. The icons used to display battery status are shown in Figure 22-1.

You might also see an icon for a dead battery, but for some reason I can't get my tablet to turn on and display that icon.

Battery is fully charged; the tablet is happy.

REMEMBER

Heed those low-battery warnings! The Galaxy Tab alerts you when the battery level gets low, at about 15 percent capacity.

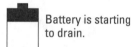
Battery is starting to drain.

Another warning shows up when the battery level gets seriously low, below 5 percent — but why wait for that? Take action at the 15 percent warning.

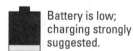
Battery is low; charging strongly suggested.

- When the battery level is too low, the tablet shuts itself off.

TIP

- The best way to deal with low battery power is to connect the tablet to a power source: Either plug it into a wall socket or connect it to a computer by using a USB cable. The tablet begins charging itself immediately; plus, you can use the device while it's charging.

Battery is very low; stop using and charge at once!

Battery is charging.

Figure 22-1: Battery status icons.

- You don't have to fully charge the tablet to use it. When you have only 20 minutes to charge and you get only a 70 percent battery level, that's great. Well, it's not great, but it's far better than a lower battery level.

TECHNICAL STUFF

- Battery percentage values are best-guess estimates. The typical Galaxy Tab has a hearty battery that can last for hours. But when the battery meter gets low, the battery drains faster. So, if you get 8 hours of use from the tablet and the battery meter shows 20 percent left, those numbers don't imply that 20 percent equals 2 more hours of use. In practice, the amount of time you have left is much less than that. As a rule, when the battery percentage value gets low, the battery appears to drain faster.

Determining what is sucking up power

The Galaxy tablet is smart enough to know which of its features use the most battery power. To check it out for yourself, open the Settings app. Tap the General tab, and then choose Battery from the list of items on the left side of the screen. You see the Battery screen, similar to the one shown in Figure 22-2.

The number and variety of items listed on the Battery screen depend on what you've been doing between charges and how many apps you're using.

Carefully note which apps consume the most battery power. You can curb your use of these programs to conserve juice — though, honestly, your savings are negligible. See the next section for battery-saving advice.

- ✔ You can touch any item listed on the Battery screen to see further details for that item. On the Use Details screen, you can review what is drawing power. On some screens, buttons are available that let you disable features that may be drawing too much power.

- ✔ Not everything you've done shows up on the Battery screen (refer to Figure 22-2). For example, even after I read a Kindle book for about half an hour, Kindle didn't show up. Also, I've seen the Gallery app show up from time to time, even though I didn't use it.

Current battery charge and state   Usage and time chart

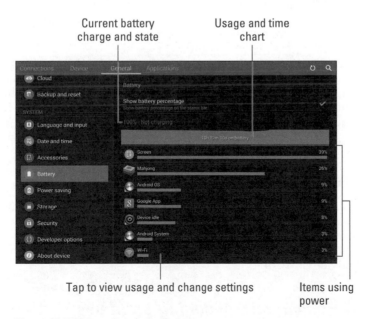

Tap to view usage and change settings   Items using power

Figure 22-2: Things that drain the battery.

Extending battery life

A surefire way to make a battery last a good long time is to never turn on the device in the first place. But rather than let you use your Galaxy Tab as an expensive hors d'oeuvre tray, I offer a smattering of suggestions you can follow to help prolong its battery life.

Dim the screen: If you look at Figure 22-2, you see that the display (labeled Screen) sucks down quite a lot of battery power. Although a dim screen can be more difficult to see, especially outdoors, it definitely saves battery life.

Adjust the screen timeout: Make the screen sleep at a shorter interval to save valuable battery life. Or manually lock the tablet, especially if you're just listening to music. See Chapter 19 for information on display settings.

Turn off vibration options: The tablet's vibration is caused by a teensy motor. Although you don't see much battery savings by disabling the vibration options, a minuscule savings is better than no savings. See Chapter 19 for information on disabling vibration options.

Lower the volume: Consider lowering the volume for the various noises the tablet makes, especially notifications. Information on setting volume options is found in Chapter 19.

Turn off Bluetooth: When you're not using Bluetooth, turn it off. See Chapter 16 for information on Bluetooth, though you can turn it off easily from the Quick Actions at the top of the notifications shade.

You'll find a Power Saving item in the Settings app (look on the General tab). Select the item on the left side of the screen. Then touch the Master Control by Power Saving Mode to activate the feature. In this mode, the tablet itself makes subtle adjustments to prolong battery life. Also available is Ultra Power Saving Mode, which applies even more restrictions.

Help and Troubleshooting

Wouldn't it be great if you could have an avuncular, Mr. Wizard type available at a moment's notice? He could just walk in and, with a happy smile on his face and a reassuring hand on your shoulder, diagnose the problem and tell you how to fix it. Never mind that such a thing would be creepy — getting helpful advice is worth it.

Fixing random and annoying problems

Here are some typical problems you may encounter on your Galaxy Tab and my suggestions for a solution.

General trouble

For just about any problem or minor quirk, consider restarting the tablet: Long-press the Power Lock button and choose the Restart command from the Device Options menu. Tap the OK button. This procedure will most likely fix a majority of the annoying problems you encounter.

Signal weirdness

As you move about, the cellular signal can change. In fact, you may observe the status icon change from 4G LTE to 3G to even the dreaded 1X or — worse — nothing, depending on the strength and availability of the cellular data service.

My advice for random signal weirdness is to wait. Oftentimes, the signal comes back after a few minutes. If it doesn't, the cellular data network might be down, or you may just be in an area with lousy service. Consider changing your location.

For Wi-Fi connections, you have to ensure that the Wi-Fi is set up properly and working. This process usually involves pestering the person who configured the Wi-Fi router or, in a coffee shop, bothering the cheerful person with the bad haircut who serves you coffee.

Perhaps the issue isn't with the tablet at all but rather with the Wi-Fi network. Some networks have a "lease time" after which your tablet might be disconnected. If so, follow the directions in Chapter 16 for turning off the tablet's Wi-Fi and then turn it on again. That often solves the issue.

Another problem I've heard about is that the Wi-Fi router doesn't recognize the Tab. In this case, it could be an older router that needs to be replaced. Especially if you have a Wi-Fi router over five years old, consider getting a newer router.

Music is playing and you want it to stop

It's awesome that the tablet continues to play music while you do other things. Getting the music to stop quickly, however, requires some skill. Primarily, you need skill at pulling down the notifications shade and tapping the Pause button that appears in the currently playing song's notification.

An app has run amok

Sometimes, apps that misbehave let you know. You see a warning on the screen announcing the app's stubborn disposition. When that happens, touch the Force Quit button to shut down the app. Then say, "Whew!"

To manually shut down an app, refer to Chapter 18.

You've reached your wit's end

When all else fails, you can do the drastic thing and perform a factory data reset on your Galaxy Tab. Before committing to this step, I recommend you contact support as described in the next section.

Refer to Chapter 20 for details on the factory data reset.

Getting support

You can use two sources of support for your Galaxy tablet. For LTE Tabs, the first source of support is your cellular provider. The second source, or the only source if you have a Wi-Fi tablet, is Samsung. Or if you were suckered into a long-term service agreement at some Big Box store, perhaps you can try getting support from it.

Before you contact someone about support, you need to know the device's ID: Open the Settings app. Tap the General tab, and then choose About Device on the left side of the screen (and at the bottom of the list). You'll see the tablet's model number, as well as the Android version.

On my Galaxy Tab S 10.1, the model number is listed as SM-T800 and the Android Version is 4.4.2. Look up the names and numbers for your tablet, and then jot down that information right here:

Model number: 1 _____

Android version: 2 _____

For app issues, contact the developer: Bring up the app's description screen in the Play Store app. Scroll to the bottom of the screen and choose Send Email.

For issues with the Play Store, contact Google at `support.google.com/googleplay`.

If you have an LTE tablet and are an active mobile data subscriber, you can get help from the cellular provider. Table 22-1 lists contact information on US cellular providers.

For hardware and other issues, you have to contact Samsung. The support number is 800-726-7864. The Samsung support website is `www.samsung.com/us/support`.

No one likes wading through bottomless automatic customer support systems. Odds are good that you merely want to speak to a human. I've found that the fastest way to do that is to keep pressing the zero key after you phone into the system. This technique eventually turns you over to a live person who, I hope, can either deal with your problem or connect you with someone who can.

Table 22-1	US Cellular Providers	
Provider	**Toll free**	**Website**
AT&T	800-331-0500	www.att.com/esupport
Sprint Nextel	800-211-4727	mysprint.sprint.com
T-Mobile	800-866-2453	www.t-mobile.com/Contact.aspx
Verizon	800-922-0204	http://support.vzw.com/clc

Valuable Galaxy Tablet Q&A

I love Q&A! Not only is it an effective way to express certain problems and solutions, but some of the questions might also cover things I've been wanting to ask.

"I can't turn the tablet on (or off)!"

Yes, sometimes a Galaxy Tab locks up. I even asked Samsung about this issue specifically, and the folks there told me it's impossible for a Galaxy Tab to seize! Despite their denial, I've discovered that if you press and hold down the Power Lock button for about 8 seconds, the tablet turns off or on, depending on which state it's in.

I've had a program lock the Galaxy Tab tight; even the 8-second Power Lock button trick didn't work. In that case, I waited 12 minutes or so, just letting the tablet sit there and do nothing. Then I pressed and held down the Power Lock button for about 8 seconds, and the tablet turned itself back on.

"The touchscreen doesn't work!"

The touchscreen requires a human finger for proper interaction. The tablet interprets the static potential between the human finger and the device to determine where the touchscreen is being touched.

You cannot use the touchscreen when you're wearing gloves, unless they're specially designed, static-carrying gloves that claim to work on touchscreens.

The touchscreen might also fail when the battery power is low or when the tablet has been physically damaged.

I've been informed that there is an Android app for cats. That implies that the touchscreen can also interpret a feline paw for proper interaction. Either that or the cat holds a human finger in its mouth and manipulates the app that way. Because I don't have the app, I can't tell for certain.

"The battery doesn't charge!"

When your battery isn't charging, start at the source: Is the source providing power? Is the cord plugged in? The cable may be damaged, so try another cable.

When charging from a USB port on a computer, ensure that the computer is turned on. Most computers don't provide USB power when they're turned off. Also, some USB ports may not supply enough power to charge the Tab. If possible, use a port on the computer console (the box) instead of a USB hub.

"The tablet gets so hot that it turns itself off!"

Yikes! An overheating gadget can be a nasty problem. Judge how hot the tablet is by seeing whether you can hold it in your hand: When it's too hot to hold, it's too hot. Or if you're using your Galaxy tablet to cook an egg, it's too hot.

Turn off the tablet and let the battery cool.

If the overheating problem continues, have the tablet looked at for potential repair. The battery might need to be replaced. As far as I can tell, there's no way for you to remove and replace the battery in a Galaxy Tab.

Do not continue to use any gizmo that's too hot! The heat damages the electronics. It can also start a fire.

"It doesn't do landscape mode!"

Not every app takes advantage of the tablet's capability to reorient itself horizontally and vertically. For example, many games set their orientations one way and refuse to change, no matter how you hold the tablet. So, if an app doesn't go into landscape mode, that doesn't mean anything is broken.

Confirm that the orientation lock isn't on: Check the Quick Settings on the notifications shade to ensure that the Screen Rotation item is on; otherwise, the screen doesn't reorient itself.

Part V
The Part of Tens

Enjoy another Part of Tens chapter online at www.dummies.com/extras/samsunggalaxytabs.

In this part. . .

- Discover ten tips, tricks, and shortcuts.
- Work with ten things to remember.

23

Ten Tips, Tricks, and Shortcuts

In This Chapter

▶ Viewing apps in Multi Window
▶ Sleeping in with Blocking mode
▶ Making things private
▶ Using the Toolbox
▶ Employing the Smart Screen
▶ Activating the dream feature
▶ Removing the vocal dirty word filter
▶ Changing TV channels with the tablet
▶ Finding the Task Manager
▶ Monitoring online data access

A *tip* is a small suggestion, a word of advice often spoken from experience or knowledge. A *trick,* which is something not many know, usually causes amazement or surprise. A *shortcut* is a quick way to get home, even though it crosses the old graveyard and you never quite know whether Old Man Witherspoon is the groundskeeper or a zombie.

I'd like to think that just about everything in this book is a tip, trick, or shortcut for using a Galaxy Tab. Even so, I've distilled a list of items in this chapter that are definitely worthy of note.

Make Some Multi Window Magic

Samsung Galaxy tablets feature a unique multitasking feature called Multi Window. It allows you to view two apps side-by-side on the touchscreen. This is opposed to how apps normally run, which is full screen.

Before you can use Multi Window, ensure that it's activated. The quick way to turn on this feature is to pull down the notifications shade and choose the Multi Window Quick Setting. If the icon is green, the feature is active.

The Multi Window card appears on the side of the screen, as shown in Figure 23-1. To summon it, swipe right-to-left, starting at the far right edge of the screen.

After a while, the Multi Window card goes away. Before it does, tap a launcher icon to start an app. The app takes over the screen. For the magical part, summon the Multi Window card again and start a second app. Both apps share the screen, as shown in Figure 23-2, which illustrates the Gallery and Internet apps.

To adjust the window size, drag the Control Button Thing left or right, or up or down, depending on how the Tab is oriented. The two windows need not be equal in size.

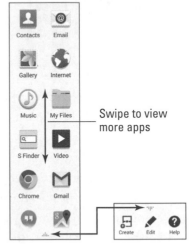

Swipe to view more apps

Figure 23-1: The Multi Window card and controls.

App window   Separator   App window

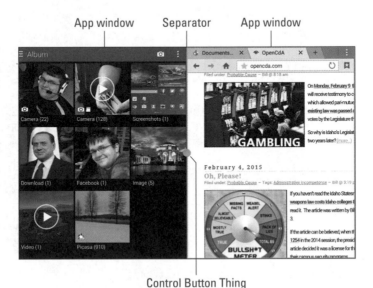

Control Button Thing

Figure 23-2: Multi Window in action.

Tap the Control Button Thing to view some additional controls. The icons for those controls are illustrated in Figure 23-3. Use the icons to swap the windows, close windows, and copy text or a screen shot between windows.

You can exit Multi Window mode at any time also by pressing the Home button.

Cycle through apps in this window

Swap app windows

Copy text or screenshot to the other window

Expand window to fill the screen

Close this window

Figure 23-3: Multi Window controls.

  ✒ Only certain apps can run in Multi Window. The variety is seen by scrolling the Multi Window card up and down.

  ✒ You can open more than two Multi Window apps. The apps keep piling up on one side of the screen or the other. Use the Swap App Windows button to pick an app for a window (refer to Figure 23-3).

  ✒ Tap the Edit icon on the Multi Window tray to add or remove apps. Refer to Figure 23-1.

Android tablets always run multiple apps at once. The only benefit to Multi Window is that you can view two apps at the same time.

Snooze Through Blocking Mode

The Galaxy Tab makes an excellent bedside clock. It functions even better as a bedside clock when you activate Blocking mode, which allows you to set a time of day when notifications and alarms can be disabled or silenced.

To access Blocking mode, obey these directions:

1. **Open the Settings app.**

2. **Tap the Device tab and choose Blocking Mode from the left side of the screen.**

3. **Slide the Master Control to the on position.**

4. **Set the start and ending time for Blocking mode.**

    For example, choose your bedtime and then wake-up time. I set my Tab for 10:00 PM and 7:00 AM. If you can't set these options, first remove the check mark by Always.

Blocking mode mutes any alarms you've set. So if you *really* need to be up by 4:00 AM, disable Blocking mode so that you'll hear that alarm.

Stay Private with Private Mode

For extra security on the Tab, you can activate Private mode. It allows you to conceal information in four apps: Gallery, Video, Music, and My Files. When Private mode is active, you can move items in those apps to a Private folder or area. Only when Private mode is unlocked can anyone see the items you've hidden.

To activate Private mode, follow these steps:

1. **Open the Settings app.**
2. **Tap the Device tab.**
3. **Slide the Master Control by Private Mode to the on position.**

   This option isn't available on the Tab 4.

4. **Enter a PIN.**

   This is a different PIN than the Lock screen PIN.

When Private mode is active, you can send items in the four apps (Gallery, Video, Music, and My Files) to the private area: View an item or long-press it and choose the action Send to Private.

As long as Private mode is active, you can view and manage items held in the Private folders. To conceal them again, disable Private mode: Follow Steps 1 through 3, but set the Master Control to the off position in Step 3.

Toolbox Button   Toolbox Apps

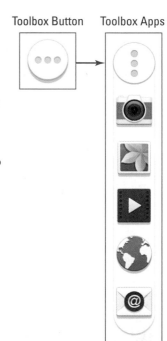

✏ You don't need to set a secure screen lock to enable Private mode. It uses its own PIN.

✏ See Chapter 20 for more information on Tab security.

Access Apps Anywhere with the Toolbox

The Toolbox feature lets you quickly access your favorite apps from a floating button that appears on every screen. The button is shown in Figure 23-4. Tap the button to view a drop-down list of apps. Tap an icon to launch the given app.

Figure 23-4: The Toolbox in action.

To activate the Toolbox, heed these directions:

1. **Open the Settings app.**
2. **Tap the Device tab.**
3. **Slide the Master Control by Toolbox to the on position.**

You see the Toolbox button, as shown in Figure 23-4. Tap the button at any time to view available apps. Tap an app launcher icon to start that app.

✔ To edit the apps, follow Steps 1 and 2, and tap the Edit icon on the right side of the screen (and shown in the margin). Use the next screen to select up to five apps for the Toolbox: Add a check mark to add an app; remove a check mark to remove an app.

✔ The Toolbox is not available for the Tab 4.

Avoid Display Timeouts with Smart Stay

Please don't be frightened, but your Galaxy Tab knows when you're looking at it. I don't believe that it actually stares back at you, but it can look for your eyeballs. The advantage is that the display won't automatically lock as long as you're looking at the Tab, providing you activated the Smart Stay feature.

Laying aside your fears, activate Smart Stay by opening the Settings app.

If you have a Tab S, tap the Device tab and then choose Display from the left side of the Screen. On the right side, place a check mark in the box by Smart Stay.

On the Tab 4, tap the Controls tab and then choose Smart Stay on the left side of the screen. On the right side, place a check mark in the box by Smart Stay.

For the Smart Stay feature to work, you must look at the screen. When your eyeballs are detected, a Smart Stay status icon appears, as shown in the margin. That icon's presence means that the feature is working.

Watch the Tablet Dream

Does a Galaxy Tab fall asleep when the screen locks? A locked tablet seems rather restrictive, so I prefer to think of the tablet as taking a snooze. But does it dream? Of course it does! You can even see the dreams, provided you activated the Daydream feature — and you keep the tablet connected to a power source or in a docking station. Heed these steps:

1. **Start the Settings app.**

2. **Tap the Device tab, and then choose Display from the left side of the screen.**

3. **On the right side of the screen, slide the Master Control by Daydream to the on position.**

   The Daydream feature is activated. Now you choose a daydream type.

4. **Tap the Daydream item to view the various types of daydreams available.**

   I'm fond of Colors.

 Some daydream items feature a Settings icon, which can be used to customize the daydream.

The daydreaming begins when the screen would normally time out and lock. So, if you set the tablet to lock after five minutes of inactivity, it daydreams instead.

- To disrupt the tablet's dreaming, swipe the screen.
- The tablet doesn't lock when it daydreams. To lock the tablet, press the Power Lock button.

Add Spice to Dictation

I feel that too few people use dictation, despite how handy it can be. Whether or not you use it, you might notice that it occasionally censors some of the words you utter. Perhaps you're the kind of person who won't put up with that kind of s***.

Relax, b******. You can lift the vocal censorship ban by following these steps:

1. **Open the Settings app.**

2. **Tap the General tab, and then select Language and Input on the left side of the screen.**

   On the Tab 4, tap the Controls tab, where you'll find the Language and Input item.

3. **On the right side of the screen, tap the Settings icon next to Google Voice Typing.**

4. **Slide the Master Control by the option Block Offensive Words to the off position.**

On the Tab 4, uncheck the box.

And just what are offensive words? I would think that *censorship* would be an offensive word. But no, apparently the words s***, c***, and even innocent little old a****** are deemed offensive by Google Voice. What the h***?

Use the Galactic TV Remote

Your Galaxy Tab features an infrared port, called the IR Blaster. It really has only one purpose: to transform your tablet into a large TV remote control. To make that transformation, you use the WatchON app.

To get the most from WatchON, you need to have an Internet-ready TV. That TV must be on the same Wi-Fi network as the Tab. After you get things connected, you can use WatchON to control the TV, set the volume, and most importantly, change channels. The app also serves as a program guide: Tap a program on the screen and the tablet switches channels on the TV.

Use the Task Manager

You may not think it's a treat, but plenty of other Android tablet users would love to have a Task Manager app. It's not really necessary to use the Tab, but it comes in handy for killing off unruly apps. In fact, if you're looking for a Quit command for any App, the Task Manager is your tool.

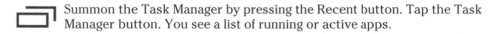

Summon the Task Manager by pressing the Recent button. Tap the Task Manager button. You see a list of running or active apps.

To switch to an active app, tap its item in the list.

To kill off an active app, tap the End button.

To kill off all running apps, tap the End All button.

 ✔ You can kill active apps also by swiping them off the Recent apps list, so that aspect of the Task Manager isn't unique. The End All button, however, is unique to the Task Manager.

 ✔ Also see Chapter 18 for information on stopping apps run amok.

Check Your Data Usage

Whether you have an LTE or Wi-Fi Tab, you can use the Data Usage screen to check Internet activity and even control how much data is sent and received.

To visit the Data Usage screen, open the Settings app, tap the Connections tab, and choose Data Usage. You see a graph charting data usage over time. LTE Tabs also feature red and orange limit bars, which you can adjust to set warnings when your mobile data usage gets too close to your monthly limit.

To review network access for a specific app, select it from the list. You'll see an overlay of the app's data usage, as well as a delicious pie chart. If you notice that the app is using more data than it should, tap the View App Settings button. You may be able to adjust some of the settings to curtail unintended Internet access.

24

Ten Things to Remember

In This Chapter

▶ Switching apps quickly

▶ Choosing Quick Settings

▶ Speaking to the tablet

▶ Locking orientation

▶ Improving your typing with suggestions

▶ Minding the battery hogs

▶ Making phone calls

▶ Checking your schedule

▶ Taking a picture of a contact

▶ Setting an event's location

*H*ave you ever tried to tie string around your finger to remember something? I've not attempted that technique just yet. The main reason is that I keep forgetting to buy string and have no way to remind myself.

For your Galaxy Tab, some things are definitely worth remembering. Out of the long, long list, I've come up with ten good ones.

Summon a Recently Opened App

An Android app doesn't quit. It stays running until it's bored and shuts itself down, you turn off the Tab, or you force it to quit. In the meantime, you can easily switch between running apps by pressing the Recent button. Choose an app: Presto! It's on the screen.

✒ The Recent list of apps is obviously important, otherwise Samsung wouldn't have put the icon right below the touchscreen.

> ✔ If you need help remembering how the Recent button works, think of it as the same thing as the Alt+Tab key combination in Windows.

Make Quick Settings

Shortcuts exist for many of the common things you do on the Galaxy Tab. Especially for those items that can be turned on or off, you'll probably find a Quick Setting.

To view the Quick Settings, pull down the notifications shade. The Quick Settings icons march across the screen, left to right; scroll the icons left and right. Tap the Grid button in the upper-right corner of the screen to view all the Quick Settings at once.

Use Dictation

Dictation is such a handy feature, yet I constantly forget to use it. Rather than type short messages or search text, use dictation. You can access dictation from any onscreen keyboard by touching the Dictation (microphone) icon. Speak the text; the text appears. Simple.

See Chapter 4 for dictation information.

Lock the Orientation

It's nice to be able to rotate the tablet, alternating between portrait and landscape orientations. Some apps look good one way; others, the other way. The rotation lock feature prevents the apps from switching when you don't want them to: The screen stays fixed in whichever orientation it was in when you set the orientation lock.

To set the rotation lock, pull down the notifications shade. In the Quick Settings area, locate the Screen Rotation item. Touch it to lock orientation. Touch it again to unlock.

Use Keyboard Suggestions

Don't forget to take advantage of the suggestions that appear above the onscreen keyboard while you're typing text. In fact, you may not even need to type much text at all: Just keep tapping a word in the list presented. It's fast.

To ensure that suggestions are enabled, follow these steps:

1. **Open the Settings app.**
2. **Tap the General tab.**

   On the Tab 4, tap the Controls tab.

3. **On the left side of the screen, select Language and Input.**

4. **Tap the Settings icon to the right of the Samsung Keyboard entry.**

   The icon is found on the right side of the screen, similar to the one shown in the margin.

5. **Ensure that the Master Control by the Predictive Text option is in the on position.**

Also refer to Chapter 4 for additional information on using keyboard suggestions.

Avoid Things That Consume Lots of Battery Juice

Three items on your Galaxy Tab suck down battery power faster than a massive alien fleet is defeated by a plucky antihero who just wants the girl:

- A bright display
- Bluetooth
- Navigation

It takes a lot of power for the tablet to give you a nice, bright touchscreen, so don't make the screen any brighter than you have to. If possible, set the brightness to Auto. That setting saves a lot of power. See Chapter 19 for more information on properly setting the touchscreen brightness.

Bluetooth requires extra power for its wireless radio. The amount isn't much, but it's enough that I would consider shutting it down when battery power gets low.

And while you may not be using navigation that often, it does use a lot of power. The Tab's GPS radio is being read and the network accessed to provide current information. Further, the display is on all the time, which causes perhaps the fastest battery drain possible.

Make Phone Calls

Yeah, I know: It's not a phone. I wish it were (and Samsung might as well), but your Galaxy Tab lacks a native capability to use the cellular system for making phone calls. Even so, with apps such as Hangouts and Skype, you can make phone calls and even video chat with others. Refer to Chapter 7 for details.

Keep Up with Your Schedule

The Calendar app can certainly be handy, reminding you of upcoming dates and generally keeping you on schedule. A great way to augment the calendar is to employ the Calendar widget on the Home screen.

The Calendar widget lists the current date and then a long list of upcoming appointments. It's a great way to check your schedule, especially when you use your tablet all the time. I recommend sticking the Calendar widget right on the main Home screen.

See Chapter 18 for information on adding widgets to the Home screen; Chapter 14 covers the Calendar app.

Snap a Pic of That Contact

Here's something I forget: Whenever you're with one of your contacts, take the person's picture. Sure, some people are bashful, but most folks are flattered. The idea is to build up your Contacts list so that every contact has a photo.

When taking a picture, be sure to show it to the person before you assign it to the contact. Let her decide whether it's good enough. Or, if you just want to be rude, assign a crummy looking picture. Heck, you don't even have to do that: Just take a random picture of anything and assign it to a contact. A plant. A rock. Your cat. Just keep in mind that the tablet can take a contact's picture the next time you meet up with that person.

See Chapter 11 for more information on using the tablet's camera. Assigning contact pictures is covered in Chapter 5.

Enter Location Information for Your Events

When you create an event for the Calendar app, remember to enter the event location. You can type either an address (if you know it) or the name of the location. The key is to type the text as you would type it in the Maps app when searching for a location. That way, you can touch the event location and the tablet displays it on the touchscreen. Finding an appointment couldn't be easier.

✔ See Chapter 10 for more information about the Maps app.

✔ See Chapter 14 for details about the Calendar app.

Index

• *U* •

• *V* •

About the Author

Dan Gookin has been writing about technology for over 25 years. He combines his love of writing with his gizmo fascination to create books that are informative, entertaining, and not boring. Having written over 150 titles with 12 million copies in print translated into over 30 languages, Dan can attest that his method of crafting computer tomes seems to work.

Perhaps his most famous title is the original *DOS For Dummies,* published in 1991. It became the world's fastest-selling computer book, at one time moving more copies per week than the *New York Times* number-one bestseller (though, as a reference, it could not be listed on the *Times*' Best Sellers list). That book spawned the entire line of *For Dummies* books, which remains a publishing phenomenon to this day.

Dan's most popular titles include *PCs For Dummies, Word For Dummies*, *Laptops For Dummies*, and *Android Phones For Dummies.* He also maintains the vast and helpful website www.wambooli.com.

Dan holds a degree in Communications/Visual Arts from the University of California, San Diego. He lives in the Pacific Northwest, where he enjoys spending time with his sons playing video games indoors while they enjoy the gentle woods of Idaho.

Publisher's Acknowledgments

Acquisitions: Katie Mohr

Project Editor: Susan Pink

Copy Editor: Susan Pink

Editorial Assistant: Claire Brock

Sr. Editorial Assistant: Cherie Case

Cover Image: Front cover: ©iStock.com/FrancescoCorticchia, ©Logan Duffy